"If the late Erma Bombeck Lisa Espinoza Johnson would have been their love child, and every mom of young children would have benefited. Erma did not marry Bill but *Days of Whine and Noses* is still the best thing that can happen to a harried mom. Lisa's insightful encouragement is wrapped in just the right amount of sharp wit and grab-your-sides humor. The Bible says that laughter is good medicine and that the truth will set your free. Open wide! *Days of Whine and Noses* has just the right dose of both."

—Ken Davis, author, comedian, grandfather extraordinaire

"*Days of Whine and Noses* not only met, but exceeded, all requirements for a 'Don't Miss This Book!' endorsement. Lisa's clever writing will have you snorting out loud with laughter, clasping your legs together in a mad attempt to control postpregnancy issues, and identifying with her real-life confessions of motherhood, children, and sanity. Don't miss this book, indeed!"

—Julie Ann Barnhill, national speaker and author; *She's Gonna Blow, 'Til Debt Do Us Part,* and *Scandalous Grace*

"Through *Days of Whine and Noses,* Lisa Espinoza Johnson has facilitated a sort of 'sisterhood of motherhood' for readers by capturing familiar scenarios from these priceless years and sharing them with plenty of humor and encouragement. If you make the time to read this wonderful work, you will find that your stolen moments were indeed well spent."

—Irene Dunlap, coauthor,
Chicken Soup for the Kid's Soul,
Chicken Soup for the Preteen Soul,
and *Chicken Soup for the Soul*
Christmas Treasury for Kids

Days of Whine and Noses

Pep Talks for Tuckered-Out Moms

Lisa Espinoza Johnson

JOSSEY-BASS
A Wiley Imprint
www.josseybass.com

Published by Jossey-Bass
A Wiley Imprint
989 Market Street, San Francisco, CA 94103-1741   www.josseybass.com

Jossey-Bass books and products are available through most bookstores. To contact Jossey-Bass directly call our Customer Care Department within the U.S. at 800-956-7739, outside the U.S. at 317-572-3986, or fax 317-572-4002.

Jossey-Bass also publishes its books in a variety of electronic formats. Some content that appears in print may not be available in electronic books.

Library of Congress Cataloging-in-Publication Data
Johnson, Lisa Espinoza, date.
    Days of whine and noses: pep talks for tuckered-out moms / Lisa Espinoza Johnson.—1st ed.
        p. cm.
    Includes bibliographical references.
    ISBN 0-7879-6881-1 (alk. paper)
    1. Mothers—Religious life. 2. Parenting—Religious aspects—Christianity.
    3. Child rearing—Religious aspects—Christianity. I. Title.
BV4529.18.J637 2004
248.8'431—dc22   2003022069

Printed in the United States of America
FIRST EDITION
HB Printing   10 9 8 7 6 5 4 3 2 1

Contents

To Chase, Chance, Chandler, and Charli:
I wouldn't trade our
Days of Whine and Noses for anything.

Acknowledgments

A book can never be written in a vacuum, though it would be fantastic if a book could vacuum, now wouldn't it? This undertaking has been a team effort, with lots of helping hands along the way, some of whom will undoubtedly escape my thinking until after this page has long since gone to print.

Julianna Gustafson has been much more than my editor. She has been my advocate, my cheerleader, my fellow visionary, my friend. From day one (literally), her enthusiasm for this book has been a constant wind in my sail. Surely, no first-time author has had such a positive experience. I consider myself to have been spoiled rotten, and now she must forever remain my editor.

If not for Carla Barnhill at *Christian Parenting Today,* I'm certain that *Days of Whine and Noses* would still be a few chapters scattered around my hard drive. Her belief in this project and in me as a writer led me to Julianna at Jossey-Bass, and for that I'm forever grateful.

There is absolutely no way on earth I could have written this book without Chip, my husband of twenty years. Practically speaking, he has critiqued chapters, untangled my computer screw-ups, and played Mr. Mom on the weekends I was away writing. His unwavering support and total disregard for limitations inspire me to believe I can do anything (except get him to pick up his dirty underwear). Without these many years of seeing up-close in Chip what grace looks like, the tone of this book would be very different. He continually pushes back the walls of my tiny universe. All that, AND he's so darn cute!

I also couldn't have written this book without Shari Johnson, for two reasons. First, she is the mother of Chip. Second, she spent many hours in these chapters—proofreading, changing phrases here and there, overhauling paragraphs. An incredibly funny and gifted writer, her instincts were always right on the money. Mom gave me completely honest feedback when my ramblings didn't make sense or when my writing was just plain bad. She also doled out large portions of encouragement that kept me going. It's great when you get a two-for-one like this.

Special thanks to Norm and Verna Shawchuck for allowing me to use their condo as a writer's retreat. Countless hours and late nights at the computer with no interruptions, sipping coffee and munching on biscotti in my PJs—I suddenly feel the need to write another book!

Thanks also to Jim and Johanna Townsend for my stay at the Townsend Inn, where several chapters took shape and I was inspired by stories from the others staying at the inn.

The folks at MOPS International have played a huge part in my living this dream. I am especially grateful to Elisa Morgan and Carol Kuykendall, under whose wings it is an honor to be cozily tucked. They have sponsored, supported, and encouraged me, and have given me priceless opportunities to live out my passion of encouraging moms.

I'm thankful to Ken Davis for helping me see my twisted sense of humor as a gift from God and to Charlene Baumbich for teaching me the importance of being true to that gift and to myself.

One of the biggest steps in this exciting journey was taken a few years ago when Aunt Cho demonstrated her unflinching faith in me. Everyone needs an Aunt Cho to help make her dream a reality.

Introduction

As I sit here writing, long after my youngest has gone to bed (the only time I can really keep a train of thought on track), I am filled with gratitude for the opportunity to connect with you, my fellow mom. Three years ago, this book consisted of two short chapters and a dream to encourage other moms in the trenches just like myself. For some reason, I felt it wasn't the right time to dive headfirst into finishing the book. I did, however, know the title, and that this book would someday become a reality. I put it on the back burner and went back to school to finish my psychology degree.

Three months after my classes started and seven years after my husband's vasectomy, I took a

test and passed—with a big blue *plus sign*. We were
going to have another baby! Lots of wonderful
details I'd love to share, but that'll be another book.
Condensed version: I finished school, giving birth to
Charlize (Charli) about halfway through and leaking
milk as I walked the graduation line, and within
three months was talking with Jossey-Bass about
this book I wanted to write, which had only two
chapters and a title thus far. God's timing is perfect.
I didn't have to dredge my memory for chapter titles.
I was living them afresh every day with Charli. Now
it was time to give birth to *Days of Whine and Noses*.

    This book is about our lives as moms. Our
days and nights are often filled with the mundane—
diapers, sticky messes, 2 A.M. feedings. Sometimes
the mundane instantaneously morphs into chaos, as
we rush to the ER with a feverish toddler or attempt
to juggle a six-year-old's birthday sleepover, a
stopped-up sink, and a dog that just dove into the
cake. Sometimes they make us laugh. Sometimes we
laugh to keep from crying. But *always,* these Days of
Whine and Noses offer us the richest lessons of life—
a deeper meaning than meets the eye.

    Don't feel as if you have to start at the begin-
ning and read the chapters in order. Skip around if
you like. Pick the chapter title that speaks to where

you are today. And take your time. Don't try to swal-
low the whole thing at one time (as if you had that
much time to sit still anyway). Read a chapter and
live with it. You may even feel inspired to pull out
your journal (or start one) and write about your own
Days of Whine and Noses.

You'll notice here and there a few references to
passages from the Bible. That's because personally
I've found my most satisfying soul nourishment, my
greatest encouragement as a mom, from scripture. It
keeps me grounded, knowing that I'm loved by God
just as much on my "If I hear the word *Mom* one
more time I'll *scream!*" days as on my "Hey, let's
make Rice-Krispy treats!" days. If that's not where
you are on your life journey, don't worry. You will
still find affirmation and inspiration on the pages
that follow.

My hope is that in reading these pages you will
be reassured that who you are and what you do as a
mom is of utmost significance and that your eyes
will be opened to the deeper meaning in even your
simplest tasks. And I hope that you laugh a lot.

Days of
Whine and Noses

On First-Time Parents

Something crazy happens in the brain chemistry of first-time parents. Neurons begin firing at a rapid rate, pulsing the message, "Germs are evil, and their mission is to invade your baby! Protect! Insulate! Encapsulate! Defeat the enemy!" (I am of course speaking of every *other* first-time parent, not myself. I was so grateful to have someone else take my screaming, colicky baby off my hands, the only requirement was to have been off probation for at least two weeks and in remission from whooping cough for one.)

My friend Stacey recently became a first-time mom. One evening, I asked if I could hold little Caleb. She replied sweetly, "Of course you can. I have wipes right here." Unsure if she was implying that I should change his diaper, I innocently queried, "For what?"

"To wipe your hands, silly." I was offended. Yes, I had just scratched my butt and picked my nose, but that was with my *left* hand and I was going to stick my *right* index finger in his mouth to suck on.

It goes something like this. First-time parent: the pacifier falls on the floor; mom rushes to disinfect it. Seasoned parent: pacifier falls to the floor; mom licks it (if anyone's watching) and sticks it back in Junior's mouth.

First-time parent: toddler drops cracker on the ground outside; mom throws it away. Seasoned parent: toddler shares cracker with family dog; mom exclaims, "How cute!" and snaps a photo.

First-time parent: only certain screened, licensed medical professionals and grandma after surgical scrub-down can hold the baby. Seasoned parent: if you're a friend or family member with no suspicious drippings, you're welcome to hold Junior. And please pass him on at your own discretion, as I will be lying down in the other room taking a nap.

The classic first-time-parent prize goes to my friends Debbie and Tom, whose three beautiful girls are surprisingly normal. Debbie and Tom were pastors of a small church in a rural community. Only days following the birth of their firstborn, Kristen, they were faced with a dilemma. The wonderful folks at church were dying to see their precious new parishioner. But Debbie and Tom knew that these well-meaning people were unwitting messengers of all manner of malicious microorganisms. They must protect their defenseless baby girl at all costs.

Like a pimpled face emerging from puberty, the answer became clear. The announcement went out to the members of the congregation, preparations were made, and the much-anticipated day finally arrived. Debbie donned her prettiest dress, put on her make-up, and styled her hair. Then she dressed little Kristen in her Sunday finest—a portrait of perfection from head to toe. Debbie and Kristen took their place in the living room, carefully assuming the consummate Madonna-and-child pose while Tom ceremoniously opened the curtains.

There with eyes of wonder stood the proud congregation. In grand procession, they filed by the picture window, oohing and aahing at the angelic presentation. The most elegant boutiques of Beverly Hills never boasted such a breathtaking display. I can just imagine the talk at the local diner: "Hey'd you see that new window display at the Cedarblom house?" "Yep, beats the heck outta that fancy ridin' lawn mower down at the hardware store." Never underestimate the ingenuity of a protective first-time parent.

Stories like Debbie and Tom's are undeniably hilarious. But at the time, those paranoid parents were dead serious. So were we. How did we get beyond the extreme, the ridiculous? Through growth and maturity, through the passing of time and the tempering of experience. In the scheme of life, we are all in the beginning stages, like first-time parents, in different areas. We are all on a learning curve of some sort. What if some zealous, seasoned know-it-all jumps in and tells us we're all wrong and we need to do things differently? Well, at the time we're probably not prepared to do anything productive about the sudden attack on our best intentions. But time and experience will help us in its own patient way if friends and acquaintances will allow nature to gently guide us back to reality.

There was a diaper commercial on TV recently about how new parents always start off buying "those expensive diapers." It ends with, "Live and learn. And then get LUVs." There are some things we learn best with time and experience, and we moms owe it to one another to bite our tongues and keep our, "Oh, you'll get over that," to ourselves. Let that young mom learn for herself that posing her baby before a picture window and keeping her hermetically sealed may be going a bit overboard. In years to come, you'll look back and laugh, and she'll appreciate a friend who knew when to let her live and learn.

On Potty Training

To potty train or not to potty train. That, my fellow moms, is *the* question. Psychologists and childrearing experts tell us we mustn't rush our little ones into the scary adult world of the giant white porcelain abyss that steals away the very substances our toddlers have so proudly produced. We should wait ever so patiently until they are good and ready before proceeding with this potentially life-altering process. So how do we know when that perfect, magical moment called "ready" arrives? And here's a frightening thought . . . what if it *never* does?

Perhaps I didn't burp them enough as babies or I fastened their diapers too snugly or I used the snot-sucker a bit too vigorously. Obviously, I had

inadvertently committed some horrible act that
stunted their development because never once did I
pick up on any discernible signals that these kids
were "ready." I grew weary of waiting. Somewhere
along the way, I experienced a profound epiphany—
I was ready and that was enough.

Determined to meet with swift and sure success in this task of housebreaking (I mean potty
training), I bought a book that promised to teach
me how to have my child in big-boy underwear by
the next day. He was. Wet, poopy big-boy underwear,
but underwear nevertheless. Not even Ninja Turtle
skivvies were motivation enough to get him to the
toilet on a regular basis.

You're probably thinking, "The poor baby was
probably just too young!" Think again. With kindergarten looming just over the horizon, I was haunted
by visions of sending him off to school with a Cat-
in-the-Hat backpack full of diapers and cash incen-
tives for the teacher to ensure her cooperation.
Eventually, they'd have to invent a whole new line of
diapers just for my family: Smart Didys—The Diapers That Grow with Your Academic Career.

After several failed attempts, at last in desperation I stumbled upon the method that ultimately
worked for all three of my boys. I told them, "Hey,

you're three-and-a half. Stop going to the bathroom
in your pants." No M&Ms, no jelly beans, no trips to
the toy store. Just a few sincere reprimands and
time-outs, and the Ninja Turtles found a dry home
at last.

Now the horrifying thought occurs to me—
what if they really weren't ready? Should I have
waited until they approached me and said, "Mom,
I'm graduating from elementary school tomorrow. I
think I'd like to try big-boy underwear now"? I pray
that I didn't harm their delicate psyches and that I
won't someday turn on Jerry Springer and see my
sons lamenting their tormented, lost childhoods
because their mother made them sit on the giant
porcelain abyss before they were ready. Oh, well. At
least they'll be wearing big-boy underwear, and for
that their wives will thank me.

Life is like potty training. We are faced with
choices to grow and change all the time. Most of the
time, it's much more comfortable to stay in our diapers, so to speak. It's easier to stick with something
we know, something old and familiar, than to move
on to something new and different, an unknown.
The reality is, change is the nature of life. From the
moment we're conceived until the moment we die,
everything about us is in a constant state of change—

the number of neural connections in our brains, our physical capabilities, our ideas and ways of negotiating life, the circumstances surrounding us.

Change can be a rewarding experience if we are willing to step forward with open arms to welcome the new possibilities before us. If Columbus had decided to stick with the safe Eastern route to India, imagine how differently history might have played out. Had Howard Schultz stayed in his safe job at a small coffee company instead of moving forward to something new and different, we wouldn't have Starbucks. And because Ann Moore was willing to embrace the possibility of change, moms the world over can enjoy hands-free shopping, courtesy of Ann's ingeniously designed Snugli baby carrier.

Is there an area of your life in which you're resisting change? Maybe you're torn between staying anchored in familiar waters and launching out into new ways of thinking or being. Picture the change before you as a door of opportunity just begging to be opened. Maybe that magical moment called "ready" has arrived. Embrace the change and see what happens. Bye-bye diapers. Hello big-girl underwear!

On Binkies

Where do binkies go to hide? No matter how large my stockpile, the day inevitably arrives when only one lone pacifier remains, and it's playing hide-and-seek. It's naptime. Life as we know it is suspended as every member of the household is commissioned in the search-and-rescue operation, signaled by the frantic call, "Where's the binky?!"

Who in the world thought of sticking a nipple on a handle to try to soothe a crying baby? I have a theory. Years ago, some exhausted nursing mom willing to do anything for a moment's peace mused, "I'll bet if I removed my nipple and let the baby suck on it for a while, I could catch a couple winks." To which her terrified husband, fearing she just may attempt to test her assumption, instantly responded, "Oh, honey, please don't do that! I've got just the thing."

Off he raced to his workbench where he snipped and twisted and hammered and glued. Back in a flash he flew and presented his grateful wife with the world's first "nipple on a ring," as he called it. Though the name and appearance have been refined, the end result is the same.

I realize it's not always politically (or perhaps I should say parentally) correct to admit to using a binky. I don't care. I've used them for four kids, and not one of those kids has gone off to kindergarten sporting a plug. They do not look like Mr. Ed and don't seem to be suffering any psychological damage, though undoubtedly some well-meaning professional will presently announce an insidious new malady plaguing our upcoming generations: pacifier dependence residual disorder.

The other evening, I took the kids out to a local family-owned restaurant for dinner since Dad was out of town. Fun was had by all, a mess made by most, but I didn't have to clean it up. So it was a good night. Upon arriving home, I carried Charli upstairs, ready to tuck her in beddie-bye and have a little quiet time to curl up with a book and a beverage, only to discover much to my horror that the last precious binky was missing!

The signal was given. The search was on. We searched the stroller, but no binky. We hunted throughout the house, no binky. We inspected all the usual depositories where previous runaway pacifiers had been located. Still no binky. For those of you who are politically correct and *cannot* relate to my panic-stricken state, replace the word *binky* with *blanky* or *lovey* or whatever item your child has adopted as a comfort mechanism. Yep, you get it now. It's missing, it's bedtime, and as we say in the South, "This dog ain't gonna hunt."

Having turned up empty-handed at home, I hopped in the car and drove back to the restaurant. Barefoot, out of breath, and wearing a look of sheer desperation, I accosted the owner-manager of San Giovanni's Restaurant: "Sir, I was here earlier tonight and I think I left *the* binky." This was obviously a man who had kids. Like Dan Rather with a breaking-news bulletin, he announced, "We have a mom here who's lost a pacifier, and it's bedtime." People shot knowing glances my way and immediately began checking beneath and on tops of tables with such fervency you'd have thought the Hope

Diamond was lurking behind the next ketchup bottle. No luck.

That dear, dear man marched to the back of the restaurant where his large Italian family was enjoying their nightly dinner gathering and made the appeal: "Does anyone have a binky we can give this young lady?" Lo and behold, his daughter-in-law reached into her diaper bag and produced a brand new binky, never before used, and presented it to me—a gift wrapped in empathy only a fellow mom can truly impart. God bless you, Mr. San Giovanni.

Binkies are a gift from heaven in my estimation. My kids all loved their binkies. Those priceless nipples on rings represented comfort and security for my little ones.

Do you have a binky? Is there something you keep just for yourself because you love it? Something that you enjoy, that brings comfort and security to you? It's so easy to get lost in the all-encompassing role of motherhood. But consider this. Before you were a mom, you were a woman. What does that woman love to do?

I love reading. If I have a book, I'm happy. The only time I had to curb my love for reading was when I had newborns, but even then I soon learned that during feedings I could prop up a book on the nursing pillow and enjoy sometimes a whole chapter per meal!

Do you love to paint? My neighbor hired a sitter for a day so she could spend some time with her brushes and canvas. Maybe coffee with friends is what keeps you afloat. Tuck the little ones in bed, put dad in charge for the rest of the evening, and make a run for the coffee shop. I have a friend who, whenever her husband is out of town for a few days, hires a sitter one evening so she can go out with friends or shopping or whatever suits her fancy at the time. Are you a scrapbooking addict like me? Put a date on the calendar once a month to spend an evening cropping with your fellow photo junkies.

What energizes you? It's worth a little planning and effort to make sure whatever that is maintains a place in your life. When you take care of yourself, you have more to give to your spouse, and you set a good example for your children. Psychologists Henry Cloud and John Townsend, in their book *Boundaries with Kids,* agree. They say, "Kids with parents who have a life learn both that they aren't the center of the universe and that they can be free to pursue their own dreams." Turns out that nurturing your-self as a person yields benefits all around.

Is it hiding under the crib? Maybe peeking from behind the toy box? Unlike the pacifiers that eventually lose their beloved places in our kids' hearts (and mouths), there are some things we never outgrow. Taking time for the endeavors that nourish us as women is one of those things. So come on now. Where's *your* binky?

On Moms and Fashion Statements

I wonder if the guy at the grocery store today meant it as a compliment when he said to my sixteen-month-old daughter, "Oh look, you've got hair just like your mother"? I'm kind of thinking no, since Charli's baby-fine hair this particular morning was undeniably suggestive of one of those little green trolls you stick on the end of a pencil and twist really fast to make his hair stand straight up. Until that point, I had been feeling rather proud of myself. I had already made a school drop-off, done business at the bank, dumped fifty pounds of shirts at the cleaners, bought special dog food at the pet store to replace the cheap kind that was making Max puke, and filled a grocery cart—all before 10 A.M.! Then he had to go and intimate that possibly I had not allotted a sufficient amount of time for personal grooming.

Since signing on as a mom, I've stepped out in public with hair issues that would have left me mortified in years past. One time I had just finished painting on bleach for highlights when the school called and said my son had a migraine. So off I went to pick him up, highlighting foil protruding at all angles from the top of my head. My greatest fear driving down the highway was the possibility of causing an alien-landing scare or disrupting cell phone service for miles around. Incidentally, by the time I waited in line behind ten bazillion other parents picking up their kids from kindergarten and drove home, my reddish-blonde highlights were more the color of freshly bleached linens.

Hairstyles aren't the only aspect of fashion that takes a turn with motherhood. After kids, our mode of dress tends to fall into one of three categories: stay-at-home wear (includes PJs, sweats, and big vacation souvenir T-shirts), going-out wear (usually entails putting on a bra and perhaps socks if weather dictates), and going-*way*-out wear (involves a baby-sitter, makeup, and possibly even dry-clean-only fabric and thong underwear).

The other day, I was made aware of the predictability of my uniform. I was putting on socks and shoes, and Charli started to cry. My son said, "That's so cute. She thinks you're leaving because you're getting dressed." This from a kid who for the first five years of his life insisted on wearing a Ninja Turtle, Power Ranger, or Batman costume to the grocery store! He comes by it honestly. According to my mother, for a significant period of childhood my favorite outfit for any and all outings was my pink bikini and red cowboy boots.

I love that about kids. They don't give a rip what anyone thinks. They pull on that Superman mask and cape, and away they go, bounding and leaping down the toilet paper aisle. Who says you can't wear mittens and earmuffs in the middle of summer? On with the tutu and the go-go boots— let's go to the mall! They're just lovin' life, oblivious to the idea that they've chosen anything less than the perfect attire for the day.

Why do we grown-ups often allow our self-image to be shaped to such a large degree by the opinions of others—sometimes complete strangers? Why do we ruminate at length over what this or that person thinks of us? There are those among us who, even as grown-ups, manage to retain the freedom of childhood to be who they are, regardless of the tide of public opinion. One of these people is my friend Charlene, a hilarious woman and incredible writer and public speaker.

Recently, I asked Charlene whether she worries that certain people in her audience may not like her particular style of humor. Her response was classic Charlene: "I do not worry about what they're thinking or how they're judging me; I strive not to judge them. I am who I am, and that's who and what they get, no matter what they're expecting—or *not* expecting." Her sentiments are echoed somewhat in the words of Rabbi Harold Kushner in his book *When All You've Ever Wanted Isn't Enough*. He says, "If our sense of who we are depends on popularity and other people's opinions of us, we will always be dependent on those other people. On any given day, they have the power to pull the rug out from under us."

Our value as an individual is not based on the fickle judgments of others. Consider the story of the dressmaker.

Once there was a dressmaker who had an idea for a very special, very unique dress she wanted to make. She pictured every detail of this dress in her mind, down to the last button and stitch. So she went into town to pick out the fabric and the thread and the trim and the lace—everything she needed to make the dress of her dreams become reality.

When she arrived home, the dressmaker cut out the material according to the pattern she had designed for this one-of-a-kind dress. Then she went to work sewing. At last it was time for the finishing touches, the buttons, the lace around the hem, and the tiny pearls, each sewn by hand around the neckline of the dress. The final stitch in place, the dressmaker held up the dress and marveled at its beauty. It was everything she'd imagined.

Now it was time to take the dress into town to the dress shop. So the dressmaker went to the dress shop and approached the shopkeeper: "I just finished sewing this dress, and I was wondering if you might carry it in your shop. I want some special young girl to enjoy wearing the dress as much as I have enjoyed making it."

The shopkeeper replied, "Why, certainly. I'd love to carry your dress in my shop. It's a beautiful dress." So the dressmaker, bursting with pride, handed her creation over to the shopkeeper. As she did so, she asked, "Madam, what do you think you will charge for my dress?" The shopkeeper answered after just a moment's thought, "I will probably price it at around fifty dollars."

The dressmaker was taken aback. "Fifty dollars?" "Yes, that's right. Fifty dollars," repeated the shopkeeper.

Astonished at the shopkeeper's disregard for the care and intricate planning that had gone into this dress, the dressmaker continued. "But this dress is a one-of-a-kind creation. I designed it myself. I spent hours stitching by hand and attending to every detail. This is no ordinary dress."

The shopkeeper responded, "It is a fine dress without a doubt. But look around you. I have many nice dresses in my shop. I believe my estimation of fifty dollars is a fair one."

There was a moment of silence. Then the dressmaker spoke: "You may charge a meager price for this dress if you wish, madam. But I made it. I know its *true worth*."

Your worth is not determined by what others say or don't say. You are of infinite value, simply because you are marked with the fingerprints of your Creator. He alone knows your *true worth*.

Good hair day, bad hair day. Who cares! Bring it on, grocery boy. I'm headed for the store, and watch out! I'm thinkin' it's a good day for the red cowboy boots and the pink bikini!

On Little Surprises

I just stepped in poop. Not the dog's this time—
Charli's. My darling angel had removed her diaper,
and I entered the room just in time to see that
unmistakable grimace on her face—the one that
says, "Mom, I'm working on a little something just
for you." Before I could scoop her up and hang her
over the toilet, she presented her gift right there on
the living room rug. I immediately sprang into
decontamination mode, all the while attempting to
keep both Charli and the dog from invading the
quarantined area.

I thought since I'd caught her in the act, the
contaminant was well confined to just that one spot,
but somehow portions of it had been transported

elsewhere and of course I stepped in it. Only I didn't know I'd stepped in it until after I'd made several trips back and forth to the laundry room and kitchen. I noticed that the sickening stench followed me wherever I went. Just what I wanted to do for the next forty-five minutes: scrub the carpet, disinfect the floor, and scrape human dung from the microscopic grooves in the bottom of my slippers with a toothpick.

The kicker is that while I was cleaning up, she pulled her diaper off *again* and peed on the couch. I didn't see her do it, but when I glanced up from my scrubbing she was wearing a look of supreme contentment as she sat grinning, her itty-bitty bottom wedged between the dripping leather cushions. Perhaps from now on I'll call her my "wee" angel. She's earned it.

A few weeks ago, as I was bathing my wee angel the phone rang. On the other end was an educator whose expert advice I needed immediately regarding one of my kids. So rather than risk a perpetual game of phone tag, I took the call and continued getting Charli ready for bed. When the time came to slap on the diaper, I could tell she was going to give me some *loud* flack (Charli, not the lady on the phone), so I chose to leave her *au natural* and quietly playing as I continued to glean from this woman's wealth of experience.

Sometime during the conversation, I glanced over toward the dresser and thought, "Where did Charli get that big rock?" The satisfied look on her face and the sudden assault of the strong smell on my nostrils disclosed the truth: this was no rock. I shrieked into the woman's ear—this woman with whom I was attempting to carry on an intelligent conversation, this woman whom I so highly respected. I *shrieked* in her ear!

Despite my loss of composure, I regrouped and continued the serious brain-picking session while cleaning up the poop and bathing Charli for the second time. Not five minutes later, despite all attempts to maintain some air of dignity, a less-than-surprised shout echoed across the hall from my fifteen-year-old, "Mom, Charli peed all over my room!" Thank goodness this was a fellow mom who in all likelihood had experienced her own wee angels along the way.

The funny thing is, when you encounter these sorts of incidents frequently enough, you grow somewhat unsurprised by the surprises. Like the day my husband went to grab something out of the fridge and casually called out, "Who pooped in the kitchen?" You forget that in many homes interrogatives like my husband's would never be uttered, that these most basic of bodily functions are rarely open to public display or discussion. They are, in many homes, contained within a specially designated cubicle. Having little ones around yanks us right out of the cubicle, or out of the box, so to speak.

When babies are in diapers, they haven't yet learned that there is only one proper depository for all things excremental. Thus for a toddler to see what his or her very own body has produced sitting right in the middle of the kitchen floor is not an offense but rather a natural study in the boundlessness of creativity. I find it absolutely charming and delightful that, given no preconceived notions of what goes where, these little ones throw open the doors of possibility and exploration!

Turns out, this bent toward creativity has been wired into us right from the get-go. From technicolor birds, black-and-white-striped quadrupeds, and neon fish to golden deserts, sapphire oceans, and marshmallow clouds above—all of nature is testament to a masterful Creator who wants his kids to carry on the family tradition.

We are fulfilling a God-given purpose when we use our skills, our hands, our imaginations to leave our own unique, indelible mark on the day. How do you express your creativity? Have you ever put together a scrapbook page? Made up a lullaby for your little one at bedtime? Thrown a pinch of this, a teaspoon of that, and a whole cup of the other into the mixing bowl to come up with your own secret killer brownie recipe? That's exercising your natural gift of creativity. Yours may not look like your friend's creation or your neighbor's creation. It doesn't matter. It's *your* creation. Enjoy the process. Appreciate the outcome.

When it comes to creativity, our best teachers live right in our own homes. Let the next little surprise that greets you be your cue to jump out of the box, throw open the doors of possibility, and join the little people who naively follow in the footsteps of their "out of the box" Creator.

On Teething

It's not hard to spot a teething baby. They have that telltale perpetual string of slimy drool, not just your regular old run-of-the-mill drool but the kind that looks (and feels) like something that might have oozed from a Star Trek alien. They gnaw relentlessly on *anything* they can maneuver into their mouths and have been known to wreak more havoc on crib railings than a hundred armies of termites. They are usually accompanied by a mother with a dazed look, spent from the endless days and nights of Cranky Teething Baby Syndrome.

By the way, why is it that no pediatrician (except those who are moms) will admit that babies sometimes get fever and diarrhea with teething? It's happened with all four of mine. Coincidence? I think not.

Moms will try anything to soothe a teething baby. The first line of defense is usually to pop something frozen into their mouth—a carrot, a banana, a shoe—anything that they can vigorously gnaw on for a while. There's the ever-popular squishy teething ring with colorful fishies inside that (contrary to manufacturer's fine-print instructions) most of us have been sticking in the freezer for added effectiveness. There are numerous gels, creams, and homeopathic potions—*some* that work *part* of the time, *none* that work *all* of the time. The old standby Tylenol was the closest thing to sure-fire relief that I ever found.

Retail managers unselfishly do their part by making sure the baby aisle is largely devoted to items with bumps, ridges, and various other textures that offer a magical mouth massage to those in teething distress. And since happy gums mean a happy baby, we buy one of every kind. By the time I had my fourth, they had come up with—get this—a vibrating teether. It didn't seem to do much for the itchy gums, but it was great family entertainment watching Charli's amusement at the *bzzzz-bzzzz* sound emanating from her mouth as she bit down on the neon-green star.

Teething can indeed be a real pain. Teething at thirty thousand feet in the air is horrid. Once, on a plane to Texas to attend my nephew's wedding, I was desperate to bring some relief to my son, whose gums looked like the top of Mount Saint Helen's just before eruption. The tried-and-true over-the-counter ointments fell short of their "instant relief" claims. And you can only give a child so much Tylenol, Mylicon, or Dimetapp before you're at the end of your rope.

I overheard the two guys behind me ordering Jack Daniels whiskey, and suddenly I remembered a teething tip I'd received from a veteran mom. Under normal circumstances I would have hesitated to try it, but these were not normal circumstances. I did a 180 in my seat and asked, "Can I please have what's left of your Jack Daniels?" The startled look in their eyes alerted me to the fact that these guys thought I was coming on to them. "It's for my baby." Startle turned to disgust. "He's teething. It's to rub on his gums to numb them."

Once they understood the situation, they were more than happy to oblige. They filled their cups and graciously handed over those remaining precious drops—my last hope. At last, relief! At least I think so. It's hard to recall much after I passed out from the whiskey (just kidding).

As an interesting side note, rumors of a possible alcohol problem with Pat's sister from California ensued when my son, unbeknownst to me, dug the empty Jack Daniels bottle from the diaper bag and left it in plain view at the church where the wedding was held. Word to the weary: "Always toss your empties, moms."

Teething is a natural process. It's also a frustrating one. It doesn't happen in an instant, as much as we'd like it to. You wish somehow you could communicate to your little one that relief is just millimeters away. If you could just coax that little culprit to the surface that's causing all the commotion, things would instantly take a turn for the better. But there's not a darn thing you can do to rush things. That glimmer of white will burst on the scene not a second before it's good and ready.

Is there an area of discomfort in your life? Something you have little control over but wish you could rush to the finish line? In the midst of our discomfort is where the greatest personal growth occurs. It will probably take some time and may happen in such small increments that you won't even notice. The oyster can attest to that. When a grain of sand irritates the oyster, a process is set into motion. Eventually, the end result of this gradual process is a beautiful pearl hiding within the oyster's shell.

Trust the process. When breakthrough comes *(and it will),* you'll find you've gained not a new tooth but new understanding, greater insight, deeper compassion, bolstered self-confidence . . . or maybe a pearl of wisdom. Now go to the mirror and smile. Just look at those fabulous pearly whites. See what comes of a little discomfort?

On Sleep Deprivation

Some people fantasize about romance, others about exotic travel. I fantasize about sleeping in. If a fairy godmother suddenly appeared and offered me the opportunity to wave a magic wand and change anything about being a mom, I wouldn't have to think twice. Ask anyone who lives in my house. I'm not a nice person when I don't get my sleep. Actually, it would be more accurate to say there is a list of nasty words my kids are not allowed to use that could adequately sum up my temperament when operating on too-little sleep.

Significant portions of my cerebral tissue cease to function when I'm running on sleep deprivation. Once after a *long* night with my newborn daughter, I was on the phone with the insurance company. They asked for my insurance ID number, which I promptly and efficiently rattled off. There was a pause, and then the voice at the other end of the line informed me, "Ma'am, that's our phone number." As if *she* were the one who'd said something stupid, I replied, "Well, then I guess it's not my ID number, now is it?"

I remember vividly the night almost sixteen years ago when sleep as I knew it ceased to exist. The sun went down, bedtime approached, and I fervently anticipated slipping off into uninterrupted slumber. I tucked our brand new baby boy into his cradle and crawled into bed. No sooner had I said hello to Winkin' and Blinkin' when the cries of an irritable infant broke the sound barrier in the Land of Nod. We ate, we bounced, we rocked, we swayed. We ate, we swayed, we bounced, we rocked. We cried. What we did *not* do was sleep. The next night was no better, nor the next or the next. It would be months before bedtime signified something other than Mommy-and-me Olympics and an all-night all-you-can-eat buffet.

By the way, do *not* have your credit card handy while walking the baby at 3 A.M. Every infomercial known to man airs from midnight to 6 A.M. They know we're up walking the babies, and there they are, ready to sell us the latest gadgets guaranteed to flatten our abs, remove that unwanted facial hair, and store six months worth of homemade baby food in just one tiny two-ounce jar. You don't know how close I came to owning a zit sucker/car vacuum.

It's true a mother never sleeps the same as she did before kids, but once they're older, it's the exception rather than the norm to be awakened by a sick six-year-old or a fussy fifteen-year-old—and virtually never by a nine-year-old who wants to nurse (though just last week I was awakened almost simultaneously by a fifteen-year-old with a stopped-up nose and an eleven-year-old with a throbbing ingrown toenail that I instinctively removed with the skill of a surgeon, eyes half-shut). So when Charli came along eight years after my youngest son, I was yanked right out of the season of the "good night's sleep" and transplanted back into the season of "Good *night!* Would you *please* sleep!"

I've talked to plenty of moms who say the newborn stage is their favorite part of mothering. To those stalwart women I say, "Are you *nuts?*" For me, the whole newborn thing (all four times) is largely a blur because of that nonfunctioning cerebral tissue issue. Apparently, there are some people for whom sleep deprivation is a minor inconvenience. A small dab of concealer here and there and voila! Good as new. For others of us, it's more like being stranded on Gilligan's Island, ever hoping for that elusive helicopter to swoop down and carry us back to civilization. Thankfully, the day of rescue always comes. One morning we open our eyes to the light peeping through the window and realize we've slept an entire night! The helicopter has landed and whisked us off to the land of the living.

It's all about hope. Though your last uninterrupted night's sleep may date back before the dinosaurs (Barney and Baby Bop that is), the blessed eve will arrive. Though you can count on your big toe the number of hours you've snoozed in the past three weeks, your time is coming. Though you're considering trading in your bed for a more useful piece of furniture (say a Peruvian basket-weaving loom), sleep will *not* forever elude you.

How do I know? I know because I've lived it. Four times in my life I've lamented with all certainty, "I will *never* sleep more than three hours in a row again." But I clung drowsily to the hope that one bright and beautiful morning I would join the ranks of the sufficiently slumbered. And sure enough, four kids later I'm sitting here wide awake at my laptop, typing with all certainty: you *will* sleep again. Hold on to hope.

Have you ever tried to define that word *hope?* Without going to a dictionary I mean. I'll admit, as I sit pondering my next tap of the keyboard, I struggle to wrap words around this concept of hope. It's almost easier to just stick it in a sentence and draw out the meaning from its context. "I *hope* I pass my driver's test." "I'm *hoping* for a speedy recovery." "This marriage counselor is our last *hope.*"

We don't say, "I *wish* so" but rather, "I *hope* so." We don't have "high *wishes.*" No, it's "high *hopes*" that fuel the audacity of the itsy-bitsy ant to even dream that he could take on the proverbial rubber tree plant. Sometimes we link the term with a partner: "hopes *and* dreams" or "hopes *and* prayers."

This notion of hope—it evades even Webster's best attempts at explanation. But our hearts comprehend full well what our words fail to adequately capture. We know we need hope. It moves us from a place of inertia to a place of vitality. It's the "Don't give up" whispered in the ear of the faint of heart, the "It ain't over 'til it's over" nudging the weary and wiped-out to take another step.

But what if circumstances dam up the river of hope? What if we've dredged the bottom and come up dry—not a drop of hope to be found? A man named Paul, who wrote much of New Testament scripture, scraped through some pretty bleak and seemingly hopeless scenarios (imprisonment, beating, shipwreck, to name a few) and found a wellspring of hope—an inexhaustible geyser that gushes up from the parched riverbottom. In an incredibly encouraging letter, Paul offers this blessing to some friends in Rome: "Now may the God of HOPE fill you with all joy and peace in believing, that you may ABOUND in HOPE."

That's it! There's the geyser! Regardless of circumstances, statistics, projections, or any other external impositions, hope just keeps bubbling up because God is its source, and God is infinite. Certainly breathes new life into that old saying, "Hope springs eternal."

What circumstance are you in right now that seems hopeless? How would your outlook change if you trusted that God has an infinite supply of hope for that situation? You won't be in this place forever. So do you see a helicopter flying around up there? Who knows, tonight could be the night of the big rescue. Here's *hoping!*

On Oozing Poop

It was a damp, frigid winter day (as damp and frigid as it gets in Southern California), and two-year-old Chase and I were on our weekly supermarket safari. Almost at the end of my list, I was meandering through the produce section when an unpleasant odor drifted my way. Continuing to shop, I assumed my little guy was just having a wee bit of gas. The odor, however, didn't seem to dissipate but instead to become more and more pungent. I had to face reality. We had a poopy on our hands.

I quickly discovered this was no ordinary poopy. As I looked over the cucumbers, I saw it out of the corner of my eye. There it was on the left side of my cart by the handle: the poop blob. In a flash of motherly instinct, I grabbed for a handful of plastic produce bags and threw them over the evidence. In retrospect, I could recall receiving a few awkward glances from fellow produce shoppers. Now I knew why.

When my turn came in the checkout line, I pushed my cart through to the bag boy, who saw my son and instinctively got that "Cootchie-coo" look about him—for about one second. Gagging, he turned his attention to rapidly bagging my groceries, carefully avoiding contact with the blob. I assured the checker I'd be taking their cart to the bathroom and washing it off, which I immediately endeavored to do.

Upon my arrival in the restroom, I surveyed the situation and discovered that the diaper's contents had traveled up Chase's back and onto his neck, and had somehow made its final exit onto the cart. After cleaning the mess from around those tiny bars of the cart as best I could with a wet paper towel, I moved on to the source of the toxic spill. Oozing poop means poopy pants, poopy shirt, poopy socks, poopy shoes. I removed the clothes and was about to delve into the hub of the matter when I discovered that my diaper bag was void of both diapers and wipes.

Out into the store I careened like Mario
Andretti, straight to the baby aisle to grab the necessary items and back to the bathroom, thankfully
avoiding any collisions. I carefully and creatively
removed the overflowing diaper, wiped all cracks,
crevices, and appendages, and covered that clean little bottom with a fresh didy, all without benefit of a
changing area. Now having spent enough time in
the store to receive employee benefits, I was finally
ready to go. I thought.

It dawned on me just in time that I wouldn't
want to add a shoplifting charge to the excitement
of the day, so I once again went through the checkout line to pay for the diapers and wipes. The bag
boy kept his distance. I paid. I left.

As I passed through the front doors into the
biting cold of the evening air, the eyes of an incom-
ing shopper fixed themselves on my bare-bodied little boy. I knew what she was thinking. "That poor
child's mother should be arrested—taking him out
in the cold wind with nothing on but a diaper!" I
practically bit a hole in my tongue to keep from
blurting out, "Lady, it's *his* fault. He was *dressed* when
we got here!"

What I wouldn't have given on that cold,
poopy day for an understanding look and a heart-

felt, "Hang in there." You know what I'm talking about. You burst through the kindergarten door with Suzie ten minutes late after quelling an ant emergency back home and cleaning up the baby, who decided to remove his own stinky diaper in the crib upon awakening, only to be met with the icy stare of the teacher who can't understand what in the *world* is so hard about getting your daughter to school on time. When's the last time you longed for a word of encouragement to punctuate your poopy mommy day?

Encouragement is a powerful thing—"Like apples of gold set upon a silver platter," as the writer of Proverbs put it. The golden apples spoken of here could be the kind we buy at the store to bring health to our bodies and sweetness to our tongues. Or they could be apples *literally* made of gold. Either way we look at it, the picture painted here is one of *refreshment* and *beauty*. A word of encouragement is *refreshment* for a weary soul, a moment of *beauty* in the midst of a trying day.

This week, practice being an encourager. You won't have to look far for an opportunity to plant a big fat golden apple in the middle of a silver platter. Start with those right in your own home. Maybe your husband had a setback at work or your little one lost his favorite Hot Wheels car. Then as you go about your errands at the bank or the post office, be on the lookout for "golden apple" opportunities. Undoubtedly, you'll cross paths with someone along the way who could use a little mom-to-mom understanding—perhaps the stranger in line at the grocery store with two screaming toddlers. Your encouraging words could provide just the boost she needs—the fresh-scented baby wipe to her oozing poop day. How do you like them apples?

On *La Décor des Bébés*

I used to say, "When I have kids, I will *not* rearrange my entire home just for them. They will learn to adjust." I also said I'd never wear bell-bottoms again, but I just bought a pair. There's no denying it. The presence of little ones has a distinct impact on even the most sophisticated of decorators, transforming elegant, serene homes into technicolor ads for Toys "R" Us.

I have a friend whose home was the epitome of charming country decor: dolls of every shape and size, stuffed critters, pillows, and an assortment of knick-knacks to rival that of the finest country boutique. Even the little dolls playing marbles in front of the fireplace were perfectly posed, each marble

purposely positioned for maximum cuteness. Once
her daughter hit the toddler years, my friend's deco-
rating taste seemed to take a sudden, drastic turn.
She sold the entire country collection at a garage
sale and adopted the mode of décor chosen by most
mothers of young children known as *la décor des
bébés,* adding appropriate Fisher-Price, Playskool,
and Little Tikes pieces along the way.

Sometimes you forget that not everyone shares
your appreciation for *la décor des bébés.* Last week, I
happened to visit a friend in my neighborhood who
has the same floorplan as we do and whose two children are well past the preschool years. Oddly, her
house and mine look nothing alike. I was surprised
that she had opted for a table and chairs in the for-
mal dining area rather than the Little Tikes swing
and slide combo and the kitchen playset that seem
to fill the area nicely in my home. Flanking her dramatic spiral staircase is an ornate buffet, while I've
chosen a primary-colored pop-up tent for that particular space. Near the entryway is a lovely marble
cocktail table graced by an elegant floral arrange-
ment. My coffee table is adorned at the moment by
an *I Spy* Christmas picture book, a half-eaten candle,
and a stuffed reindeer that sings "Jingle Bells."

I realized one day how accustomed I'd grown
to *la décor des bébés* when a friend called my attention

to the dog's leash dangling capriciously from the stairs. Upon recollection, it had been there several weeks and I hadn't so much as thought to ask which child had hung it there or why or even to take it down, because, after all, whoever put it there probably had a good reason.

For those interested in mastering *la décor des bébés,* there are only a few basic guidelines to follow. White or light furniture or carpet is a no-no. Go for leather or dark patterns, unless you find a light pattern that resembles the colors of the foods most often eaten in your home. Install gates or other barriers at the bottom and top of stairs; ours is stylishly attached with leather belts. Obstruct the view from above and below with heavy mesh netting attached to the banisters. Place some type of large rolling toy (scooter, dumptruck, and so on) in every room of the house. Find a cute basket, fill it with diapers, wipes, and Desitin, and place it intentionally beside the couch in a classic display of art that proves once again that beauty need not be sacrificed to function in *la décor des bébés.*

Replace glass objects d'art and floral arrangements on coffee tables with cardboard pop-up books and talking *Sesame Street* characters. Never paint over the well-scrubbed remains of the magic marker self-portrait on the kitchen door. Toss some blocks here and there for ambience, and always keep a stroller parked beside the front door. Perhaps the most important rule in *la décor des bébés* is this: you can never have too many neon-colored plastic accessories. If a guest enters your home and is greeted by the sight of a lime-green toy lawnmower and a biohazard-orange wagon, you have masterfully achieved the desired effect. You will burst with pride as he or she exclaims, "Ah, *la décor des bébés!*"

Each of us has our own personal décor—the décor of our life. It's called character, and it's what people remember about us. Maybe it's your honesty that strikes people. Maybe they are drawn to your ability to laugh at yourself and make others feel comfortable with your humility.

My sister-in-law is a remarkable person. The thing people remember about her is that no matter who you are or what you do in life—maid, mother, or magistrate—you walk away from any encounter with her feeling special. Some people are known for their strength of conviction. Others inspire and encourage those around them to move toward goals and dreams to which they never imagined they could aspire. My husband is like that. He's the reason I can write this book. Some individuals are marked by a steady perseverance that keeps them plodding along, even when the winds of circumstance blow right in their face. My sister, a single mother of two, is one of those people.

Something about you becomes settled in the memory of every person you meet. It's more lasting and significant than just your cutting-edge hairstyle or your knack for putting together the perfect fashion ensemble or even your flair for *la décor des bébés*. A part of *who you are* sticks with them. Are you kind? Optimistic? Generous? A good listener? Like the unmistakable geometric lines of a Little Tikes play kitchen greeting guests as you welcome them into your home, something about your character makes a lasting impression. So, girlfriend, what's your décor?

On Buying Time

I want to go on record as saying a great big "Thank you!" to the inventors and manufacturers of feminine hygiene products. You have played a key role in my personal appearance on numerous occasions. Because of you, I have looked presentable and even (dare I say?) glamorous for family portraits, holiday events, and dinners out with my hubby. Who would have guessed a maxi-pad could wield so much power? Yet that little adhesive-backed strip of protection can keep my one-year-old occupied for thirty minutes! Yes, thirty minutes! That's long enough to get dressed, dry my hair, apply makeup, and even accessorize my outfit.

The other day, my fifteen-year-old son came into my room while I was getting ready for a Christmas party. He found me in my bathroom, floating in a sea of unwrapped tampons, maxi-pads, and pantiliners. The crazy thing is, he's so accustomed to such a sight that it didn't phase him in the least. He simply asked, "Mom, have you seen my drum key? I think Charli took it." "Yes, son, I believe it's underneath the pile of pantiliners." Which begs the question, "Are sanitary products still sanitary once they've been unwrapped, chewed on, and scooted across the floor?"

Every mom can name at least one questionable, if not downright unorthodox, distraction that buys her that extra five minutes to finish the dishes or ten minutes to pay the bills. Another of Charli's favorites is to dip each nugget of the dog's food into his water one by one and then feed it to him. It's messy and is probably a tremendous stressor for the dog, but the benefit is at least five minutes to finish the task at hand. Others include unfurling a roll of toilet paper, coloring on herself with a marker, and unloading the wastepaper basket. Mom's tolerance for each particular distraction is in direct correlation to her motivation level to finish the impending task.

A sure sign that Charli has begun to employ alternative methods of entertainment is the unusual silence that ensues. That typically means she has wandered into the pantry and is quietly grazing. In all likelihood, she has tipped over the Cheerios or dumped out the Cheez-Its and is feasting like a queen. I'm aware that she could be consuming more than her share of Girl Scout cookies. And she may very well be feeding Max . . . one Corn Pop at a time. This could keep her busy for ten minutes—fifteen if Max doesn't get sick of Corn Pops. Meanwhile, I'm scribbling out the last of the checks to be deposited in the mailbox before the mailman arrives.

Another sure-fire distraction is my set of keys. No matter how many "realistic" sets of keys I buy at the toy store, she always prefers the real deal. She uses them to start the couch, her toy ride-on car, the TV. They'll usually buy me at least five minutes—ten if she doesn't set off the panic button first.

Sometimes we moms have to buy time in order to accomplish the necessities of the moment (and sometimes the well-deserved little luxuries). However, because of some maternal genetic coding, the cost of buying time bears a big, fat price tag reading *Guilt* (note the capital G). We feel *guilty* if we don't accomplish *anything,* and we feel *guilty* if we accomplish *something* because we let things slide a little with the munchkins.

It seems that guilt is an inevitable accompaniment to motherhood. Why is that? Well, I think the guilt often comes from a ridiculously unrealistic expectation we impose on ourselves—to *always* have *everything* under control, in other words, to be *perfect*. "I *should* be able to pay these bills *and* keep her out of the pantry." "I *should* stop mopping up the spilled milk and take the dripping toilet plunger away from Junior." "I *should* have gotten up two hours earlier so I could make homemade cookies for the preschool party."

Here's a *should* for ya. To borrow a term from many modern-day psychologists, we *should* stop "shoulding" on ourselves. Constant guilt over what we're doing wrong renders us incapable of appreciating what we are doing right.

I've always faltered under the June Cleaver standard where the pillows on the sofa are symmetrical, the casserole's in the oven, and the reprimands are in a whispered tone. She was perfect, and I . . . well, let's just say my kids prefer making forts with the pillows, the mac'n'cheese is in the microwave, and I do yell at them to cease and desist whatever mischief they're concocting, though I usually follow it with "please." Perhaps it's age, or just as likely fatigue, that has led me to sign my own permission slip—the one that says, "Lisa Espinoza Johnson is hereby allowed to be human (that is, to be perfectly imperfect)." When we let ourselves off the hook, so to speak, we are freed up to actually enjoy being moms.

Perhaps you are lucky enough to be sitting down with a cup of coffee as you read these words, but only because you put little Sarah in the playpen with some animal crackers and a bottle. It's OK. See that price tag with the big letter "G" dangling from your well-deserved and much-needed moment of relaxation? Right now, grab the scissors, *cut off* the *tag,* and enjoy the tradeoff!

On Colic

Whoever comes up with the cure for colic will go down in history as the richest person to ever live. Though the exact *cause* of colic is a matter of much speculation, its manifestation can best be summed up in the following acrostic:

C—Chronic
O—Outrageously
L—Loud
I—Infantile
C—Crying

A mother's first encounter with the term *colic* usually comes shortly after baby's homecoming.

Mommy looks forward to hours of gazing into her little one's eyes or watching her sleep, only to be surprised instead by hours of unremitting wails. She calls up her mom, the pediatrician, or some more experienced friend and relates her quandary. The voice on the other end of the line responds, "Sounds like your baby's got colic." Which really means, "Suspend all previous expectations of motherhood, stock up on coffee—and by the way, I hereby rescind my previous offer to babysit."

You can always spot the moms whose babies aren't quite living up to that "bundle of joy" epithet. They carry bags under their eyes big enough to store a dozen diapers, drive aimlessly around the neighborhood at odd hours, and listen with bewilderment and envy as other moms (obviously much *better* ones) punctuate their conversations with, "Jenny's such a good baby," and "Isn't it wonderful being a mom!"

I wish someone had told me before giving birth to my first child that a large portion of this baby's first few weeks, nay months, would be spent screaming for no apparent reason. Not that I could have done anything about it, but at least I could have adjusted my expectations a bit. Shortly after Chase was born, my best friend (who had *no* children at the time) veritably bubbled as she asked me, "Do you just *love* being a mom?" Never one to mince words, I replied, "I'll get back to you on that." I couldn't figure out for the life of me which part of mothering was supposed to be so wonderful. Was it the sleep deprivation, the endless crying (the baby's and *mine*), or the complete lack of routine?

It wasn't until later, when my pediatrician finally told me my son likely had colic, that I discovered not everyone's baby has the same knack for noise as mine. Apparently, the gene runs in our family, for only one of my babies was born minus "the gift."

To be honest, I was quite relieved to have a label attached to this craziness. I wasn't a horrible mom after all. "So what do we do about it, doc?" I asked. Hope loomed on the horizon. He looked at me as if I'd asked for ET's phone number. "You can't *do* anything about it. He'll outgrow it in a few months." Little did he know that he had just peeled all ten of my white-knuckled fingers off the ledge from which I had been dangling and sent me plunging hopelessly downward.

In my quest for quiet, I tried every "remedy" that came across my path—the baby seat on top of the washer trick, the baby in a sling while you vacuum trick, the stinky herbal tea trick—everything but the eye-of-newt, wing-of-bat trick (only because the drug store was always fresh out of newts). Driving around the neighborhood for hours sometimes helped. The dilemma was always, do I stop the car and risk him waking up or keep driving until he's two?

We also found a miracle in a bottle called Mylicon. When it worked (which happened about 30 percent of the time), it was incredible. The doctor told us, "It's perfectly safe. You can use it anytime." So at the first sign of distress, we'd grab the Mylicon, praying that this would be the time it did its magic. The problem was that it came in a .000014-ounce microscopic bottle that cost like fifty dollars when they should have made two-gallon economy-size jugs with a convenient pump dispenser.

Retailers know exhausted moms will pay any cost for a few minutes' calm. They tantalize us with products sure to quiet the fussiest of babies—a teddy bear with a freakishly loud heartbeat ("just like mom's"), an outboard-motor-type contraption that makes the crib vibrate like a car badly in need of a tune-up, and a plethora of "soothing" bath products, including baby massage cream. I tried them all.

(By the way, I bought the massage cream, but no one offered to give me a massage.)

One night in desperation, I snatched up practically an entire aisle at Babies "R" Us in the frenzied search for something that would calm this continuously crying kid. They knew I was coming, and they were ready. Dozens of strategically placed boxes displayed photographs of quietly content babies lounging, rocking, vibrating, and swinging. I loaded up my cart, the promise of a couple of peaceful hours just a credit card swipe away. Would you believe it? All those pictures are *fake*. They are *phony,* I tell you. Those babies are actors! After all that trouble to buy the stuff and put it together, not one of them gave my screaming baby that "I'm so happy I think I'll just drift off to sleep for hours" look I saw on the boxes.

Thankfully, everyone who told me this mysterious malady known as colic would eventually just disappear was right. Each of them outgrew the screaming-meemie stage, only to pick it back up again at about age two, and then again to some extent at age fourteen.

As a brand new mom with a constantly screaming baby, for the first time in my life I stared straight into the face of my own weakness, loss of control, and profound need. I resonated with the words of my then seven-year-old son Chance in a letter of apology to the teacher for his part in a skirmish at school. His little fingers scrawled in closing, "I need someone even wiser than my parents! I don't know how to stop it!" He needed help from someone bigger.

A long time ago, a man named Solomon had become king over the entire nation of Israel. He was in a sense hanging off the ledge by two fingers, overwhelmed at such a monumental responsibility. He, like Chance, acknowledged his need for help from someone bigger. History records Solomon's prayer: "My God. . . . I'm too young for this, a mere child! I don't know the ropes, hardly know the 'ins' and 'outs' of this job. . . . Here's what I want: Give me a God-listening heart so I can lead your people well. . . . For who on their own is capable of leading your glorious people?" This king who cried out for help from someone bigger is known today as one of the wisest rulers to ever live.

The "someone bigger" who heard and answered a desperate king nearly three thousand years ago hears the cries of a mother's heart today. "God, I feel like a child myself, and yet you've entrusted me with the tremendous privilege and responsibility of caring for these little ones. I can't do it alone. Help!"

Are you tired of trying to live up to the Supermom myth? Are you bent low beneath the burden of "having it all together"? There is strength and comfort in finally relinquishing the need to know all, to be all, to do all, in looking to someone wiser with limitless resources . . . in trusting someone bigger. Come to think of it, I'll bet he even knows what causes colic.

On Sex After Kids

My husband said to me today, "I think your flannel pajamas and fuzzy socks are sending a message." He's absolutely right. Actually, they're sending a couple of messages. First, I want to be warm and comfy. And second, we have four kids—remember, Romeo? No matter what message I *want* to send, the presence of offspring prohibits me from prancing around in the Victoria's Secret strips of cloth and string my husband has so unselfishly purchased for me through the years—the ones that convey *the* message he is *always* delighted to hear.

In pre-kid years, *the* message was sent via choice of underwear. Was it the ones with droopy elastic and gaping holes or the fancy new ones I just got at Wal-Mart? These days *the* message is conveyed pretty much in one easy-to-interpret manner. Is it Saturday night, and am I still awake?

It's that small matter of physical and emotional exhaustion from taking care of kids all day that dampens the sparks of romance. After all, if I don't have the energy to floss, how on earth am I going to scrounge up the energy to be a love goddess? Forget oysters or a glass of wine. For me, the most potent aphrodisiac is my husband making some sensuous statement like, "Honey, I just vacuumed and took out the trash." One night in an attempt to lure my husband into picking up his scattered clothes and depositing them in the hamper, I proposed in all honesty, "Consider it foreplay."

OK, since it's just us girlfriends being honest, I'll admit that I fudged a bit on the doctor's prescribed period of postpartum abstinence. "Honey, we only have to wait a little while longer, until my next check-up—in three months." The two priorities during that time were sleep and more sleep, and sex would take precious time from either one.

Nursing a baby presents its own set of obstacles in the passion department. There are only two options: wear a bra and nursing pads (which always enhances the sense of intimacy) *or* enjoy the dermatological benefits of a milk bath. Either way, reality sinks in deep. Things won't be quite the same for a while.

The issue of timing is one of the biggest barriers to sex after kids. Once in the heat of the moment, my husband and I heard a little voice just outside our locked bedroom door saying, "Bam Bam is strong." I'm not sure why my son felt the need to come and share that bit of Flintstones trivia at that particular moment, but be assured that the mercury quickly dropped on the passion thermometer. Almost every couple with kids has experienced it. Lost in the throes of ecstasy, oblivious to all but the beating of two hearts in love, you realize you're not alone. The door is open, and there is a little person standing in the doorway. Silence. How long has he been there? How much do we have to explain? Will he need therapy after this? Will *we* need therapy after this? Will we *ever* have *sex* again?

In an honest attempt to create a sensual, memorable Valentine's Day dinner for my hubby, I devised a clever plan to be carried out after the kids were in bed. I put notes all over the house leading my prince charming to the chamber of love—our bathroom. It was the only place I could think of where we'd be uninterrupted—where there would be two locked doors between us and the kids, with no little fingers probing underneath accompanied by, "What are you doing in there?"

I put cheesecake and sparkling cider on the side of the bathtub and threw a blanket over the toilet to disguise the true nature of our little love nest. The tiny bathroom was aglow with candles when Romeo arrived at last. It was all so romantic—sipping on cider, soaking in a fragrant tub, nibbling on cheesecake—until the romantic, glowing candles began sucking up all the oxygen and we started hyperventilating, not to mention sweating like pigs. It was not a pretty sight, but at least it was private.

I think we women *need* kid-proof barriers between the rugrats and the rendezvous. Our built-in wiring prevents us from operating in Mom mode and Passionate Lover mode simultaneously. At the least hint of a tiny intruder, a woman's Passion-control button switches to the OFF position in order for the Mom-control button to immediately engage. Not so with the typical male. His button simply switches momentarily to PAUSE and immediately back to PLAY the instant Little Johnny takes a step back toward his room.

Case in point. My friend Nancy and her husband, Mark, who had a preschool-age son at the time, were taking care of one of their son's little friends while his mom was in the hospital having another baby. This particular night, their son's little pal came sleepwalking into the master bedroom, making his grand entrance during a steamy reenactment of the blockbuster *Body Heat* starring Nancy and Mark. Nancy scurried into her robe and put the little guy back to bed, declaring upon her return to the boudoir, "I'm done." Passion button switched to OFF. Mark on the other hand, nonplussed by the pint-sized visitor, had switched back into PLAY mode. Apparently, it is possible to override the system because almost nine months later Nancy gave birth to *twins!*

Believe it or not, sex after kids is quite a fitting metaphor for relationships in general. Just as it takes planning and effort for physical intimacy to occur, the emotional intimacy of friendships or between family members likewise requires an investment of time and energy—an investment that yields a rich reward of meaningful connections. We all need those kinds of connections in our lives, those folks who know us "warts and all" and love us anyway.

Sometimes that soul mate is a spouse. For some it is a sister, a neighbor, or a long-time friend. Whatever the nature of the connection, it's important to carve out time together, to catch up, to laugh, to cry, to just *be*. As C. S. Lewis once said, "People who bore one another should meet seldom, people who interest one another, often."

It doesn't have to be a monumental event, maybe just a twenty-minute girlfriend-to-girlfriend phone conversation or a quick cup of coffee together. Or maybe it's a romantic candlelight lunch with your sweetie with the shades drawn while the neighbor takes your little ones to the park. They all say the same thing: "I set aside this time for us to be together because I value our relationship." The result—closeness, warmth, security, intimacy.

FYI: Regarding men and physical intimacy, the following addendum is in order. Flannel PJs override all other messages *unless* flannel PJs are accompanied by brand new underwear, absent any holes or droopy elastic, in which case the wearer of the PJs and new underwear could be accused of sending a *mixed* message. In the case of a *mixed* message, the new underwear will hold more weight than the PJs. So choose your bedtime attire accordingly.

On Perpetual Messes

Journal entry 1–7–96

Chandler, my dear Chandler. You exhaust me. Within a one-hour period of time (during which my mild headache became severe) you put *all* the towels in the bathroom into your bathtub full of water. I had to wring them *all* out and wash them. While doing that, you went into the bathroom (after being put quickly and abruptly to bed by yours truly) and put soap suds all over yourself. I angrily, as my head pounded, washed you off in the sink and put you to bed again. Five minutes later you screamed/cried down at me, "I pee the bed mom."

Journal entry 7–27–96

> I *must* document the messes that have begun to
> pervade everyday life around here. In a period of
> two weeks here's what's happened. Chandler, you
> poured marshmallows out, poured Rice Krispies
> out, spilled three glasses of pink lemonade on
> various parts of the carpet, attempted to water
> my silk plants—with apple juice—had too many
> juice spills to recall, and colored your scalp
> magenta with a marker. Chase, you fell asleep
> with gum in your mouth, and you and Chance
> woke up screaming because you were all sticky.
> Gum was everywhere! You caked chocolate syrup
> on the kitchen chairs and table and various
> places on the carpet. I'm sick of messes!

There's no denying it: life's messy. Overflowing
toilets, tipped-over trash cans, spilled coffee. Add
some kids to the mix (particularly those of the preschool variety), and the mess potential soars to new
levels. There's just no matching the mess-producing
capabilities of a two-year-old on a mission.

It would seem logical that the worst messes
would yield the most noise in the making, but indeed
the opposite is true. Whenever it gets quiet—beware.

A concentrated and intense mess is in process that will require some serious cleanup. Think about it. How much noise does a black permanent marker make? Or a tube of red lipstick? Or a dollop of Desitin? We lost a nice pair of cowboy boots to that pasty white substance that stubbornly refuses to budge once it's been smeared onto something.

Another killer mess is coffee grounds. Not a sound emanated from the pantry the other day, as Charli dumped, doodled, and delighted in the black, dirt-like remains of our morning pot of relaxation she'd pulled from the trash. Also on the list of silent messes is the mural on the wall above the crib created during naptime with only the contents of Michelangelo's diaper.

Even family pets get in on the silent-but-scary action. Last week, the kids ran downstairs yelling, "Dad, Max killed something and dragged it in your bedroom!" How much therapy will be required to reverse the psychological damage to my sons who were forced to face the shocking truth: "Guys, Max didn't kill something; that's from your *mother.*" Not a sound was made as "Maxi Pad" ripped, chewed, and tore his way to a well-deserved nickname.

Messes are frustrating because they are *never* on our "to do" list. We can't check them off with a feeling of satisfaction. They intrude on our time and obscure any visions of "productivity." It seemingly requires little or no effort to render the monstrous mess, while the cleanup can keep you mopping, scrubbing, disinfecting for hours—even days!

My theory is that messes are a sign of life. They *will* happen. Apparently, there is a principal of physics that backs me up on that. The law of entropy says basically that everything in the universe tends to move toward disorder. It just happens naturally. For things to return to a state of order, energy must be expended. Moms knew that long before it became the law of entropy. It's called the law of Pick Up Your Toys!

Sometimes we face different kinds of messes, those not so easily cleaned up with soap and a scrub brush. We've all heard the phrases. Some of us have said them. "It was a messy divorce." "My life's a mess." "I've made such a mess of things." We all have messes to deal with.

So how do we deal with them? We actually do have options. We can curse and rant and rave, disturbing everyone around and wasting precious "energy" that could be channeled toward the cleanup process. We can ignore the mess and just hope it will go away. We can point the finger of blame at someone else, leaving the mess right where it is until they admit fault and clean it up themselves (which may *never* happen). If we leave the mess lingering long enough, we'll probably step in it and carry it with us wherever we go.

Or we can stop kicking ourselves and acknowledge that messes are not unique to us. *Everyone* who is breathing has them. Don't let a mess throw you for a loop. Take some deep breaths, review your options, and commence with the cleanup. And don't hesitate to ask for help if it's just too big a mess to tackle alone.

Remember the law of entropy (a.k.a. the law of Pick Up Your Toys)? Next time you're greeted by a doozy of a mess, don't be surprised. Look at it simply as a reminder that you are alive and well on planet Earth.

On Bathroom Matters

Never in my prematernal life did I imagine that going to the bathroom would someday become a spectator sport. How could I have dreamed that such private business would in due time become a social event and, what's even more surprising, that I would actually come to think of this state of affairs as normal?

It almost becomes second-nature: herding everyone into the bathroom and proceeding with personal matters, encircled by a group of wiggling toddlers, all the while engaged in 360-degree surveillance in order to ensure that curious little hands remain outside the range of operations. Following Phase I and Phase II, Phase III entails the flush, the closing of the lid (quickly), the group exit, and the shutting of the bathroom door. Mission accomplished. Who'd have thought that this mundane process to which we barely give a second thought could hold such grand fascination for our munchkin counterparts!

In our home, simply being in the bathroom with the door shut carries no implications whatsoever. It is completely plausible to carry on a conversation about dinner options or to guide a search for the missing football from behind closed doors. I've even had homework assignments passed to me under the door for approval.

Showers and baths, once leisurely, relaxing, and *private,* likewise take on a more social tone once kids come along. I must admit, showering or bathing with Charli is becoming quite a treat these days, but before she was able to sit up, it was a major undertaking (albeit a necessary one if I was to maintain any vestige of personal hygiene). I would bathe both myself and Charli with her no-tears baby shampoo (infusing my hair with that ultra-sexy Johnson & Johnson fragrance), holding on to her slippery, soapy body with one hand and scrubbing both her and myself with the other. I suspect this will soon become an Olympic event.

You'd think with older kids it would be different. You *would* think that—*unless* you had older kids. The other night, I decided to treat myself to an unhurried warm shower after putting Charli to bed. I was just about to enter that luxurious time after lathering up the shampoo where you stand with eyes closed, motionless like a statue under the hot water for a really long time and forget there are dirty dishes to wash and clothes still to fold before bedtime.

My plan was thwarted instantly as the bedroom door swung wide open and a little person of the male persuasion (not my husband) came beebopping inside. When Chandler saw that I was in the shower, he hit rewind and backed into the hallway. I knew, however, that he had not returned to his room to wait for me to finish my long, leisurely shower because I could see the tension on the doorknob. He was going to stand outside my door, hand on the knob, poised to make his grand entrance the moment I emerged from the shower.

Seeing that there was obviously some matter of great importance at hand, I quickly rinsed my hair, savoring the last few drops of hot water, stepped out of the shower, and threw on my robe. "What is it, son?" I called, expecting some news about the urgent state of affairs between him and his brother or a report on some newly discovered mess Charli had made in his room. In he bounded, enthusiastically announcing, "Mom, guess what? If you turn out the lights and rub your hands really hard on your pants legs, you can see sparks!" I can certainly see why I had to cut my shower short for that news.

Not everyone has this kind of unfettered access to my most private moments. My kids are special. They know that there is an "open-door" policy (or a through-the-closed-bathroom-door policy) where mom is concerned, no appointments necessary. Sometimes they need something, and sometimes they just want to hang out with me. Either way, here I am, because after all, they're my children and I love them.

I'm glad that nine-year-old Chandler thought I would be elated to hear about the electrodynamic discovery involving his pants. I welcome the familiarity and intimacy that ushers my eleven-year-old to the threshold of my bathroom to ask through the door, "Mom, do you want to play Scrabble?" He's my son, and I love him so much.

The story is told that when John F. Kennedy was serving in the White House, his children could often be found sitting on their dad's lap in, of all places, the Oval Office. Though he was most assuredly a very busy man, there were some little people who, by virtue of their relationship to the president, were extended an open-door policy. While heads of state and world leaders gained audience with President Kennedy by appointment, his own children simply marched right in to see Daddy. Of course, not everyone was granted that kind of executive privilege. But they were his children, and he loved them so much.

We, in a sense, are granted executive privilege as well. You would think that God, whose job description far outweighs that of even the president, would be much too occupied to turn an ear to the concerns of a tired mom. Turns out, just the opposite is true. The heavenly Father who calls us his own children actually *wants* us to ask him for help whenever we need it. He isn't bothered by our intrusion into his personal space. He invites it!

God swings open his door to you and me and says, "Come on in anytime. I'm always here for you." Why on earth would he invite such intimacy? Why would he desire our lives to be in continuous connection with him? Just because we're his daughters, and he loves us so much. Talk about open-door policies!

On Labor Discomfort

One of the stupidest statements I have ever read was in my college psychology textbook. The writer spouted, "The pain of childbirth is due more to fear than to actual physical causes." Go ahead and read it again. It's just as stupid the second time around. Apparently, this brilliant author's protégé was my first Lamaze teacher, who said, "It's not really labor *pain* . . . just *discomfort*." Getting your fingers smashed in the door of the minivan is discomfort. Having your hair stuck in the conveyor belt at the grocery store is discomfort. Perhaps if you think swallowing a bowling ball and then passing it would constitute discomfort, then the assertion is indeed correct: pushing a small human from your loins simply causes discomfort.

In order to properly prepare for the potentially uncomfortable process of birthing our first child, my husband and I attended Lamaze class with fifteen other similarly naïve couples. He even conceded to my pleas that he wear what I thought to be an adorable show of support: a surgical scrub top that said "COACH" on the back and "Go honey, go!" on the front. My coach almost fainted during the birth videos and repeatedly begged me to allow him to sit in the waiting room like the dads in the good old days. But he hung in there, and we graduated, confident that we could handle any discomfort that might arise.

Then the big day came. After figuring out that I had not wet the bed but was in fact in labor, we headed for the hospital. For the next couple of hours, I laughed and joked with my husband and the nurses quipping, "This is a piece o' cake."

Out of nowhere, like a stab of gas from a bad burrito, the first major contraction hit. My humor was dampened for a moment, but I would regain my composure and fly through this with ease. Then another strong contraction. Then another, stronger still. My head spun around a couple of times and I turned to my husband, who was engrossed in a rerun of *The Love Boat*. With a glare comparable to Linda Blair in *The Exorcist* I seethed, "Turn that off, NOW!"

The next few hours are a blur. I remember lots of moaning and groaning and the bones of my husband's hand cracking within my grip. The word *discomfort* is about as accurate a description of what was happening in my body as would be the term *pothole* to describe the Grand Canyon. That Lamaze teacher had flat-out lied to us.

When the nurse finally said, "OK, you need to push, honey," I responded, "But it hurts to push." In a tone that conveyed almost humorous amusement at my observation, she replied, "Of *course* it does, honey." I don't know if I've ever wanted to poke someone's eyes out so badly as I did at that moment. My friend Sylvia can relate. When hard labor seized her body and Sylvia became quite vociferous, the nurses in the Catholic hospital tried to calm her: "Just breathe. It will be OK." Sylvia shot those nuns a look that could melt an igloo and hissed, "How would *you* know?"

By this time in the process I, like all laboring mothers, had instructed my husband to never again utter the words, "*we* are pregnant" because, in fact, there is only *one* pregnant person in this room and it *ain't* the guy saying, "You're just not doing the breathing right, sweetheart." This is also the time when all possibility of future romantic activity is summarily dismissed.

I remember at one point saying in all serious-ness, "I'm done. Can you just take him out now?" They were extremely unaccommodating to my request, forcing me to keep pushing for two and a half hours until my first son finally made his entrance with the help of a big toilet-plunger-looking thing that sort of sucked him out. Then there were the stitches and the abdominal massages and having to go pee for the first time. People say you forget the pain of childbirth. Maybe they mean if you fall off a building and crack your head open.

I have an aversion to pain. I don't like to expe-rience it, and I don't like to see my kids experience it. Recently, I gained a new perspective on pain from a doctor whose goal was to *help* his patients *feel* pain. Dr. Paul Brand, who worked for years with leprosy patients, has seen the devastating effects of a malady in which nerve endings are destroyed so that the suf-ferer no longer experiences pain. Parts of the body are lost due to wounds such as burns and pressure injuries because the sensation of pain does not alert the patient. He says of people insensitive to pain, "Ninety-nine percent of them have some sort of malformation or dysfunction, simply because their pain network has not been working properly."

Writer Philip Yancey, who spent a great deal of time with Dr. Brand and in fact partnered with him to write *The Gift of Pain,* gained a new perspective on this most unwelcome of gifts. He reflects, "I accept it as a signal alerting me to attend to a matter that needs change. I strive to be grateful, not for the pain itself, but for the opportunity to respond, to form good out of what looks bad."

I still don't like pain. I won't sign up for it when they pass around the clipboard. But I know it's an inevitable part of life, and I see it differently now. Pain, whether physical or emotional, is a healthy response that calls our attention to something we may otherwise ignore to our own detriment. I realize that if I allow it to, pain can shape my character, teach me compassion for others, and even bring me closer to God as I recognize his desire to comfort me in my suffering. I know that for all the pushing and panting and sweating and groaning, there is a purpose. Sometimes the purpose even has a name—like Chase, Chance, Chandler, or Charli.

On Family Vehicles

One of my favorite movies is *Jerry McGuire*. In one scene, Jerry, a sports agent, and his pro-athlete-client Rod Tidwell have a conversation in which Rod asks newlywed Jerry why he got married. Tidwell, a confirmed romantic, is less than impressed with his reply:

Jerry: Loyalty. She was loyal. . . . It just grew from there.
Rod: That's an answer?
Jerry: That's the answer.
Rod: It's not sexy.

Let's face it; family transportation is not sexy. Have you ever heard someone say, "Look at that hot minivan!" or "Man, I wish I could get behind the wheel of that station wagon"?

Though the rectangular exterior lines of the family vehicle relegate it to the "functional" category of transportation, the interior scores even lower on the "hot" scale: petrified french fries lodged under the car seat, sticky goo from a 1998 soda spill spawning life-forms in the bottom of the backseat cupholder, along with stale Cheerios and pieces of broken Happy Meal toys scattered randomly from bumper to bumper. Just this week, I found a toilet bowl brush underneath the seat (don't ask; I have no idea). Add to that the necessities—stroller, backpack, diapers and wipes, baby toys, books, Kleenex, snack container, extra binky, blanky—and you've pretty much covered every square inch of the interior.

There are also the extraordinary types of family vehicle messes that take specialized training to tackle. On the night of his eleventh birthday sleep-over (a misnomer if there ever was one), my son Chance got a migraine. The prescription medication that usually worked was doing absolutely nothing for the jackhammer in his head, so we loaded him in the front seat of the loyal family van and headed for the emergency room.

I had just pulled onto a busy street when Chance said, "Mom, I feel like I'm going to throw up." That said, Chance began a hurlfest to end all hurlfests. It was everywhere—on top of, beneath, and between the seats, inside the seatbelt buckles, covering the floor, and splattered in all directions. The next day, I assaulted the reeking mess with every heavy-duty cleaner I could find, but even after all the visible nastiness was gone, the invisible reminder lingered. This called for a professional.

My husband, bless his heart, drove that stinky van half an hour, gagging all the way, to our car dealership and had it detailed. At the end of the day, as Chip waited in line to pick up the puke-mobile, he heard people talking about how the schedule had gotten screwed up and they'd had to wait longer than usual for their vehicles to be finished. Apparently, someone had brought in a dreadfully stinky van, and it took two guys working most of the day to get the thing fumigated. I was just thankful to get my rectangle-on-wheels back home.

I need to retain that thankful attitude next time I look with a pang of jealousy at the red convertible speeding past me on the freeway. According to a landmark Harvard study on aging, *gratitude* is one key to a happier life. That makes sense. When we look at what others have and think, "Why can't *I* have that?" we automatically blur our own vision. We begin to focus on what we do *not* have rather than on the countless blessings we do have. I for one am guilty—of grumbling and complaining, of not appreciating the gifts God has given me.

Here's an exercise that helps me when my gauge reads, "Low on Gratitude." For a whole day, say a silent prayer of thanks for everything that happens, big or small, for which you are grateful. The walk to the park was warm and sunny. Thank you. The park had a bathroom, and the bathroom had a changing table. Thank you. After the park, Junior took a *two-hour* nap. Double thank you! Junior awoke from his nap calling, "Mom!" Thank you. Thank you. Thank you. Soon I find that my vision is clearer, and I can see the blessings I have on every side: family, friends, food, clothes, a home—a messy minivan.

Come to think of it, that van is quite a vehicle. It has bun-warmers built right into the front seats for those chilly Southern California mornings, adjustable cupholders throughout, and in the back are these nifty grocery bag hooks that I absolutely adore. Make fun if you wish. But last Christmas we all piled in that fumigated van, shoulder to shoulder, and made our annual pilgrimage to a local garden shop where we enjoyed the spectacular holiday light display and picked out our traditional ornament to add to the tree. Hey, it may not be sexy, but it's loyal! And for that I'm grateful.

On Mommy Talk

I'm quite certain there is a proper grown-up-sounding name for the place where we go to take care of bodily functions, but for the life of me I can't remember what it is. I still routinely ask the waiters in restaurants, "Where's your potty?"

My kids were years beyond the potty-training stage before I finally broke the habit of asking, "Do you need to go potty *in the toilet*?" That "in the toilet" part was relevant way back when, but now it seems ludicrous to anyone overhearing the exchange. "Of course they need to go in the toilet. Where else would they go?" Don't ask.

Even the most eloquent among us experiences a sudden linguistic metamorphosis upon entering motherhood. A good friend of mine, a mother of two who is always put together and on top of her game, was leaving the grocery store one evening. The checker said to her, "Good night," to which my friend automatically replied, "Night, night."

References to anatomy and bodily functions are matters about which every mother must decide her approach. Some prefer to call body parts by their actual names, while others (probably most) opt for some familiar or comfortable colloquialism such as "pee-pee," "bottom," or the ever-popular "privates."

Now the bodily functions aspect is a bit different. Parents rarely choose to use correct terminology in these situations. For instance, I have yet to hear any mother ask her three-year-old, "Honey, do you need to *urinate* or *defecate*?" Or "Sweetie, sounds like you just released some *flatulence*." I have heard grown women in public places ask their children, "Do you need to go Number One or Number Two?" This is valuable information. Number One means we may be able to make it home. However, Number Two means find a bathroom—fast!

For many budding conversationalists around the age of fifteen months or so, the word *this* takes on a world of meaning. Mother points to everything in the pantry and the refrigerator, patiently repeating, "This? This?" until Suzie finally registers a resounding, "This!" meaning, "Finally, you got it. That is exactly what I was asking for all along."

The other day, my toddler Charli picked up some innocuous household item that I really didn't want her to play with. I said, "Oooo, yucky, Charli," and she put it down. One of my older kids queried, "Mom, why is *that* yucky?" I explained to him that "yucky" doesn't just carry the conventional meaning of gross or inedible. Yucky, in the language of Charli, also means, "This is not something to throw in the toilet, bang on the floor, or put in your mouth." So now when she heads toward the boys' Playstation controllers, they proceed to tell her, "Ooo, Charli, that's yucky." They're catching on.

There have been times when I've stepped out of the world of mommy talk and attempted to communicate with my little ones on a more sophisticated level. Like the time Chase was about two-and-a-half years old and we went camping at the lake. It was midafternoon in the fly-infested, sweltering heat—conditions that exponentially increase the grouchiness factor for an overly tired toddler. After numerous attempts at getting him down for a nap, I decided to use parental logic. "Chase, you may take a nap *or* you may stay up, but if you stay up you don't get to go in the lake. Those are your two options." He adamantly announced, "I don't *want* one of those things. I don't *like* options." So much for sophisticated communication.

We forget that not everyone speaks our mommy language. One of my favorite things to do is walk around the lake, especially when Charli was first discovering animals. Every time she'd spot a dog coming her way, she'd get really excited and breathlessly blurt out, "Dah-dah." Of course, I followed with the proud announcement to the passerby with the pooch, "She loves dah-dahs!" From the looks I got, you'd have thought I was speaking Martian. "You know—dah-dahs! How hard is that to understand?"

From the earliest moments of their lives, we seem to instinctively slip into "mommy-ese" when shooting the breeze with these little people. Research actually shows that babies *prefer* the high-pitched baby-talk form of communication. Of course, at some point it is usually helpful to steer them toward complete sentences with nouns and verbs and to speak in first-person, but it turns out mommy talk is the language little ones *love* to hear.

What language do you love to hear? It floats my boat when people (and by people, I mean my husband and kids) pick up their own messes (and by messes, I mean underwear). The door to one heart may be flung open in response to a gift carefully chosen or a warm hug, while another's is opened by words of encouragement or a niche of specially carved-out time together. The concept of "love languages" has gained great popularity in recent years and for good reason. We want to communicate clearly to the wonderful people in our lives, particularly when it comes to that all-important phrase that thrills the heart and lightens the step: "I love you!"

It's the same with God. He says "I love you" in so many ways—the soft breath of a newborn baby, the warmth of a glowing sunrise, the timely word of encouragement from a friend. He even painted us a detailed picture in the life of Jesus, so we could see clearly what the language of love looks like—to embrace the outcast, to eat dinner with the undesirables, to forgive the enemy—to render meaningless the term *unlovable*. His desire is that you would never, ever doubt for one second how deeply, how passionately, how completely you are loved. That's a language we *all* love to hear.

On Runny Noses

Never could I understand why moms let their kids run around with snot dripping from their noses as if it were the most natural thing in the world. Why don't they just wipe it? What is so hard about that? Of course, that was before I had kids of my own. Now I get it. There is a principle called desensitization which means, simply stated, when you see something out of the ordinary long enough, it starts to seem normal. Those moms weren't trying to be insensitive to others and gross them out to the point of barfing. They weren't being neglectful of their children. Runny noses had become such a normal, everyday part of life, they just didn't notice them anymore.

Wanna know how to spot the mother of young children? Look at her shoulders. We moms become oblivious to the perpetual snot stains (mixed with drool) adorning the shoulders of all our shirts. We're not slobs—just desensitized.

A few weeks ago, Charli had the worst cold to date in her short little life. I marveled at the sheer volume of snot produced in that tiny head of hers. Once when she awoke from her nap completely covered in nasal slime, it was all I could do to get a grip on her to pull her out of the crib. It was most certainly this type of scenario that gave rise long ago to the clever phrase "slick as snot."

I tried to keep her nose as clear as I could with the snot-sucker (referred to by some as a nasal aspirator), but it kept flowing faster than I could coax it out. Charli's poor little nose was raw from the wiping, so I finally stopped harassing her and announced to the family, "I *know* her nose is running. Please do not *tell* me it is running. It will be running for a few days, during which time you are advised to stay out of her way and step carefully on the tile, which may be slippery in places, indeed slick as snot."

If we moms stayed home every time our kids got a runny nose, we'd be in exile for months on end. There are, however, understood hazards involved in taking a snotty-nosed kid out in public. A friend of a friend was shopping with her child one day, and, as kids will often do, he was exploring the middle of the clothes rack. When this young mom got ready to leave, her son emerged from hiding holding onto the handy handkerchief he'd discovered: the sleeve of a brand new dress shirt, now freshly slimed and shining in all its glory.

Many kids apparently find nutritional value in nasal excretions. I personally have witnessed a number of kids (not excluding my own) probe with the fervency of an archaeological dig without inhibition and then pop their findings straight into their mouths. One mom I know asked her son why he ate his boogers. She lamented ever having posed the question. His answer: "Because they taste like hot dogs."

Perhaps this nose-to-mouth connection is inborn. When she was about a year old, I taught Charli how to sign a few words in hopes that her communicative screams and grunts might morph into peaceful hand gestures. Almost immediately, she replaced the correct sign for "food" with her version, which entails ramming her index finger straight up her nostril and leaving it there momentarily.

In the adult world, snot is rarely (if ever) mentioned or dealt with to any significant degree. It's almost a nonentity. We can almost fool ourselves into thinking we are so sophisticated that no such disgusting substance would ever emanate from our bodies. Not so with little ones. Snot is as natural a part of life in the world of kids as eating play-dough and peeing in the kiddie pool.

So inherent are runny noses to the reality of little people that the color of snot is a litmus test for whether or not you can leave your kid in the nursery. Clearly posted in nurseries and childcare facilities across the world are signs in every language from Polish to Portuguese: "NO GREEN RUNNY NOSES PLEASE." The presupposition here is that kids *will* have runny noses. The question is, what color is the snot (or *discharge* as someone more discreet might choose to put it)?

The runny nose is somewhat of an icon for life with little ones. But it won't always be this way. I mean have you ever seen a seventh-grader walking around with a snotty schnozz? At some point, they either stop having perpetual nasal drips or they become socially adept enough to do something about it.

Like the falling autumn leaves that make room
for new spring growth, the runny noses will pass,
and a new season will be ushered in. Life is a continuous cycle of seasons. The temptation is to always be
looking ahead, wishing for the next season when
things will be easier, better, more productive, or more
satisfying. By living with one foot poised anxiously
on tomorrow, we rob ourselves of the ability to truly
live today. When we can learn the art of contentment
(key word here: *learn*), each new day comes to us as a
gift, wrapped up with its own unique joys and chal-
lenges, unlike any other day before or after it.

Yes, it will be easier after potty training, but
right now there's the golden opportunity to pinch
those cute little buns when the diaper gets changed.
Yes, it will be wonderful when she feeds herself, but
right now isn't it fun to sit face-to-face with this outrageously adorable, toothless dumpling and chant
"Choo, choo" as you drop the strained carrots down
the chute. And yes, it will be a glorious day indeed
when, after walking your little guy to kindergarten,
you smile and mentally review your heretofore unexplored options: cup of coffee with a friend, finish
the last chapter of the cliffhanger you've been reading, go to your favorite store and try on clothes—just

because you can. But *right now, today* you get to curl up with a little guy in his PJs and enjoy that literary classic *Green Eggs and Ham*.

Once we learn to cultivate contentment in whatever season of life we may find ourselves, we carry that contentment with us into the next season, and the next, and so on. It becomes a way of living— an attitude that refuses to trade in the value of today as a down payment on tomorrow.

So wipe them on occasion lest everyone around be grossed out. Use the handy-dandy snot-sucker on them when you must. By all means reinforce the notion that they do not contain nutritional supplements. But above all, embrace the season of the runny nose.

On Owies

I am sitting down at this moment to write as a means of therapy. Just two hours ago, I was ready to break down sobbing, but I have since then eaten half a cream-filled donut and ten pounds of toffee peanuts and am feeling much better thank you. We're out of peanuts, so now I am forced to relieve my tension some other way, so here goes.

At about noon today, Charli burned her hand on the front of the fireplace. I ran water on it, put ice on it, rubbed salve on it, all to no avail. I knew it didn't look serious enough for a doctor's visit, but I had to do something about the obviously excruciating pain. There's *nothing* worse than seeing your child in pain.

I drove like a crazy woman to the drugstore, Charli screaming the whole way, and emptied the shelves of anything that remotely resembled a pain reliever for burns. The inexpensive one with menthol she promptly rubbed in her eyes — of *course* she did, she's *one year old*. What was *I thinking?* The spray one that costs nine dollars a can, she liked. I will likely be taking out a loan in order to keep a supply on hand for the next two days, since I must reapply it every three minutes after she's rubbed the ice cube on her hand and removed the freshly applied medication.

Just as I was pulling into the garage from the drug store, my cell phone rang. I knew as soon as I heard, "This is Cathy in the school nurse's office," that I was in trouble. Before the poor woman could finish her sentence, I interrupted her, bellowing something like, "Oh crap! I don't know what I'm going to do. I have a screaming baby with a burned hand. What's wrong with Chance?" "I'm so sorry," she said in a tone that revealed her fear that the news would most assuredly deal the knockout blow to my compromised mental state. "Chance hurt his foot pretty badly playing basketball. We had to bring him to the office in a wheelchair."

The last thing I remember coming out of my mouth was, "I've got to call my husband! I don't have enough *hands*!" My mind awhirl as Charli screamed in agony from her car seat, I groped desperately to find the handles on my coping mechanism, knowing I had no choice but to hoist myself up and rise to the occasion.

How was I going to carry my screaming, aching daughter into the school and carry out my injured, aching son *and* get him to an emergency room *and* keep some ice or medicine or *something* on her hand? *How?*

In my rearview mirror, suddenly appeared the most beautiful sight I'd ever seen—my knight in shining armor. My husband, Chip, who wasn't due home until evening, came pulling up behind me in the driveway. "Help! Charli burned her hand, and Chance may have a broken foot. You take one, and I'll take the other." In a flash, Chip picked up Chance from school, performed triage, and ice-packed the ankle, while I gave Charli some Tylenol and sprayed more liquid gold on her hand.

Exhausted from the ordeal, Charli eventually fell asleep as I rocked her, holding a dripping ice cube in her throbbing, red little hand. The pediatrician just returned my phone call and declined my request for Tylenol with codeine. I was only going to take enough to calm me down. Regarding

Charli's hand, the doctor said if it's not blistered he doesn't need to see her or give her a prescription for ointment.

Chance's foot is propped up, iced, and under observation. Looks like a bad sprain, but we'll probably be in the ER (our home away from home) later just to make sure. With Charli slumbering peacefully for the time being, I am able to catch my breath and reflect on the craziness that just transpired—the brand of craziness that accompanies life with kids. It's definitely *not* the first, nor will it be the last time circumstances seem to spiral out of control. It won't be the last time I scream, "I don't have enough *hands*!"

It's hard for us moms to admit we can't do it all. Here we are in the profession that has the capacity to push us on a regular basis to the ends of our proverbial ropes, and yet we insist on trying to hang on by ourselves like a cat dangling by one claw. How many times has someone said to you, in the midst of some life difficulty, "If there's anything you need, just let me know." Did you let them know?

Tom Harken did. As a child, Tom overcame both polio and tuberculosis but fell far behind academically from missing so much school due to his illnesses. Tom eventually made it through school and worked his way into the ranks of successful entrepreneurs, ultimately owning a chain of twelve restaurants. When Mr. Harken was given the Horatio Alger Award for overcoming great adversity and achieving excellence in his field, he surprised everyone with the revelation that he had lived the majority of his life as an illiterate man. How had he been able to negotiate life and arrive at this level of accomplishment with no ability to read the written word? Mr. Harken attributes his success in large part to those individuals who came alongside to offer support when he didn't have enough hands. He puts it quite simply: "'Will you help me?' Those are the only words you need to say, and someone will help you."

Recently, we moved from our home of ten years. I was an emotional basket case. I didn't have enough hands. I called my friends. Sylvia unpacked my kitchen and fed us all for three days. Kathy came and spent the day hanging pictures, arranging furniture, and dreaming with me about the possibilities for my new home. Kristin swept my floors. When I let my need be known, good people were there to bless me with their help.

I've even come to the realization that when the bag boy at the store asks if I need help out (particularly when Charli is in tow), it's perfectly fine to look him in the eye and say confidently, "You know, my allowing you to help me to the car with my groceries is not an affront to my independence as a woman or to my competence and abilities, and it in no way diminishes the fact that 'I am strong. I am invincible. I am woman!' So yes. Yes, you may help me out with my groceries, thank you." Or you could just say, "Sure, thanks," and leave it at that.

Fortunately, there are lots of hands ready and willing to help us through those times when we reach down to grab the handle of our coping mechanism only to find that it seems to have broken off. But they can't help us unless they know we need help. Your knight in shining armor may appear in the form of sister, mother, neighbor, friend, coworker, teacher. Welcome their presence in your life. And be vulnerable enough to say honestly, "I don't have enough *hands!* Could you please lend me yours?"

On Grocery Shopping
with a Toddler

A once-routine trip to the grocery store becomes a major career move once you make that grand entrance into motherhood. Just the thought of getting the little darlings dressed, fed, and strapped into car seats with grocery list and packed diaper bag in tow is enough to make a mom rethink that whole balanced-meals theory. The wheels of creativity begin turning, and soon she's whipped up a tasty three-course meal using only what's on hand: three slices of lunchmeat, a frozen corndog, a cup of applesauce, and a can of tomato paste. BAM!

The next evening produces no such promise of a miracle meal. She must face the inevitable. Armed with a bottle of formula, a baggie of Cheerios, a

binky, and a teething ring, she embarks on her pilgrimage to the grocery store.

Following ten minutes of unloading kids and
their accompanying paraphernalia from the car and
getting everyone (except herself) comfortably situ-
ated, she is competently scanning the aisles for items
on her list. The kids both happily cooing and chat-
tering, she gives herself a mental pat on the back
just for getting here. Optimism gets the best of her,
and she actually starts out comparing prices. She
even grabs a cookie from the bakery to munch on!

All too soon, her false sense of serenity is interrupted by a familiar grunting sound coming from
Katie, who's perched in the front of the cart. Only
minutes remain before she'll be forced to make a
choice: retreat to the potty for a diaper change or
continue shopping, acting as if she doesn't smell
a thing.

Price comparisons aside, she's now randomly
hurling items into the cart. "If it's edible, we need
it," she reasons. Her speed is hindered slightly by a
vision impairment. Little Johnny, who is riding out
of harm's way in the backpack, reaches around and
explores the wonders of the human eyeball—his
mom's. She discovers that Katie has dumped her
purse and is now openly examining a feminine

hygiene product. "Katie, that is not a push-pop. Put it back now."

Down on the lunchmeat aisle, she spots a fellow mom whose little angel has grabbed a stick of bologna from the deli case and helped herself to a big bite. From the reaction of little angel's mom, she apparently hadn't been planning to buy bologna. The two moms' eyes meet in sympathetic union. Little Angel whacks mommy on the head with the bologna, the serendipitous moment passes, and they proceed with the objective at hand.

About halfway down the baby-food aisle, mom number one sustains a mild concussion as Little Johnny pulls a jar off the top shelf and drops it on her head. Only one more aisle to go and not a moment too soon. Katie, by now in all her malodorous glory, is determined to stand up in the cart, and Johnny is crying because he's tangled his binky in mom's hair.

She makes a mad dash for the checkout stand. "How are you today?" the checker queries. She forces a smile and replies, "Fine, thank you," though what she really means is, "How am I today? Hmmm . . . (binky dangling from the hair, eyes red from being poked, knot on the head as big as a golf ball)—you figure it out, Einstein." As a whiff of Katie's "aura" drifts his way, the courteous clerk loses interest and doubles his checking speed. One swipe of the debit card, all aspirations of coupon-sorting down the toilet, and she's outta there.

Why, oh why, do we do it to ourselves—pack up more stuff than most Himalayan expeditionists and enter the supermarket, always with high hopes of comparing a few prices, getting most of what's on the list (if we have a list), and arriving back home with all children in tow and all body parts in functioning order? We do it for one reason and one reason only: we gotta have food. It's a simple matter of nourishment.

Our body isn't the only part of us that needs nourishment. There's that little matter of the soul— the part of us that acts as a sort of thermostat for every other part. It's the core of who we are. If the soul is well nourished, our perspective on life comes into balance. The fuse on our temper is shorter. Our sense of optimism is renewed. We seem to laugh more easily and more often. Setbacks and messes don't seem to rattle us as much.

Let's be honest though. As moms of young children, it's no easy undertaking to carve out any kind of quiet time for ourselves. It takes effort and creativity. I know moms who've written favorite inspirational sayings or scriptures and posted them in prominent places (on the fridge, on top of the diaper pail) so they could be encouraged by them throughout the day. One friend of mine had a book of short devotionals in her bathroom so that in the *unlikely* event that she would find herself alone in there, she could treat herself to some quick inspirational reading.

Believe me (I used to be there before baby Charli came along), someday you will be able to set aside a regular time each day that's your own special quiet time, and you will be energized, renewed, strengthened, and encouraged as you grow in ways you never imagined. Until then, do what you can and don't feel guilty over what you can't.

I remember one time when my boys were very young, I left them home with Dad and went to a two-day spiritual formation seminar. People were speaking in glowing terms of the insights and growth they had experienced through deliberate focused times of contemplation and meditation. Bursting with a mixture of guilt and envy, I raised my hand and posited, "I have three extremely energetic little boys who leave me barely enough time and energy to brush my teeth. How does all this talk of the wonders of quiet time apply to me?" Richard

Foster, a gifted writer who was moderating the seminar, replied with unruffled assurance, "My dear,
your children are not an obstacle in your journey
toward God. See God in your children." Wow. The
God who gave me these energetic kids understood
my struggles and limitations. He would meet me on
my turf, my sticky, apple-juice-stained turf.

Here's my version of Mr. Foster's sage advice:
don't neglect the soul food offered to you every single day on a Winnie-the-Pooh platter. When you
push the stroller home from the park and stop to
appreciate the majesty and miracle of the sunset,
you nourish your soul. When you watch with awe
and wonder as your one-year-old scoops up a handful of sand and watches it trickle through his fingers, you nourish your soul. When you rock your
little one, breathing in the sweet aroma of Cheerios
and paradise, breathing out the prayer of gratitude,
you nourish your soul. When you hold that newborn
baby, and your heart bursts with more love than you
ever thought humanly possible, remember that this
amazing love is but a glimpse of the unfathomable,
immeasurable love God has for you. This is indeed
nourishment for your soul.

Malcolm Muggeridge said, "Every happening
in life great or small is a parable whereby God is

speaking to you. And the art of life is to get the message." Next time you're headed out to the grocery store to replenish the food supply, keep your eyes open. God just might have a message for you between the bologna aisle and the checkout stand.

On Kids and Anatomy

Having fairly well mastered Male Anatomy 101 as the mother of three sons, I found myself being dragged steadily up the learning curve when my baby-girl Charli came along. Though I had some personal working knowledge of the region, I was completely clueless when it came to the tiny, delicate parts concealed within that baby-doll-sized diaper.

Give me a quiz on circumcision after-care or how to sanitize baby-boy parts in one swipe any day and I'll ace it, but the whole baby-girl thing is very different. There are nooks, crannies, crevices, and cavities that must be cleaned with the utmost care. I had no idea how complex such a tiny tush could be. From day one I've been on the phone with friends who have daughters, nervously inquiring about some strange substance or rash that seems to appear from nowhere.

I suppose I should just call it what it is: a vagina. I don't mind using the "v" word, but sometimes it just feels funny (funny weird, not funny ha-ha), so it's good to have some back-up nicknames. I've had fifteen years to amass an impressive collection of monikers for the male appendages (not to worry—I won't recount them here). Only now, however, am I beginning to learn charming names like "pee-pee" and "tee-tee" in reference to female parts.

Some of the most priceless comments in history have issued from the mouths of preschoolers discovering that not everyone has the same plumbing. This discovery often takes place during co-ed sibling bathtime, as with my mother-in-law Shari and her brother Danny. Splish, splash, all was fun and games until suddenly a horrified Danny screamed, "Tidder (the word for sister when you can't say your S's), tidder, somebody cut off your wiener!"

Once the basic difference is revealed, the innocence of a child's mind takes over and it becomes simply a matter of fact. Sometimes trouble ensues when the child bursting with pride at this newfound wellspring of knowledge attempts to enlighten others. After a visit to New Mexico, during which Uncle Carlos (bless his heart) taught my sons a few choice words in Spanish (unbeknownst to me), I received a call from a fairly flustered first-grade teacher. "Mrs. Johnson, I'm not quite sure how to tell you this. Today Chance said something inappropriate to a little girl in class." Not *my* Chance—the perfect little student, always eager to please. "What did he say?" Did I really want to know? Her hesitancy to speak the words hinted that perhaps my son had in a moment of madness rattled off a string of profanities that would make a sailor blush. In a whispered tone she responded, "He told her that *juevos* are testicles." "Oh, my," I replied with relief. "Bilingual at such a young age!"

Apparently, Chance feels a *calling* to educate others in this regard. When he was four years old, Chance had his little friend Tiffani over to play. Tiffani had casually strolled into the bathroom while he was going potty. "You don't have a penis," he promptly informed her. "I have peanuts at home," she replied with confidence. "No, you don't have a penis." "I do have peanuts at home," she insisted. So ended the conversation. He zipped up and flushed, and off they went to play with Legos.

It's that same matter-of-fact innocence that prompted three-year-old Chandler's random observation after having walked in on Grandpa going potty. Hindered by not one iota of inhibition, he nonchalantly announced, "I have the same color pee as Grandpa. He has an alien's ding." I chalked it up to childhood imagination until a couple years later, when I learned that Grandpa had never been circumcised.

Why the vast gulf between a mature adult who can barely whisper the word *testicles* and a proud six-year-old, pleased as punch at this new bit of valuable information he wields? One word: perspective. A child views the world through unjaded lenses. Free of inhibitions, she simply and innocently experiences the wonders of her world. My point is this: the lenses we look through have a *profound* effect on how we experience life.

We've all heard the old "glass is half full or half empty" analogy. Let me put it another way. Have you ever been in a meeting when someone brought donuts (and who would have the audacity *not* to have donuts at a meeting)? You walk over to the box, praying that there'll be just one chocolate-covered donut in the bunch, but alas it appears they're all plain glazed. What loser buys all plain donuts? You pick up a fork and discreetly poke around to see which of the *plain* donuts you'll stab and put on your plate and . . . What's that? Further investigation reveals that in fact they're not all plain glazed. You flip over a deep-fried ring of dough to find rich, fudgy chocolate icing smeared all over the side that had been previously hidden from your view. Let the meeting begin. Life is good. Same donut, different perspective.

Sometimes we have to poke around a bit, flip the donut over, so to speak, to find the chocolate. The extra effort required to adjust our perspective is well worth it. It could mean the difference between a boring meeting with a plain donut and a glorious morning with a mouthful of chocolate—the difference between the embarrassment of a vociferous, anatomically informed munchkin and the enthusiasm of a budding linguist. Incidentally, I've since learned that *juevos* can also mean "eggs," as in *juevos rancheros*. I'll take mine sunny side up. *Olé!*

On Road Trips with Kids

Embarking on a road trip with kids can be compared to a dentist appointment. It's never over as soon as you'd like.

The presence of babies, as wonderful as they are, complicates any trip to the fullest possible extent—from bathroom stops, to sibling quarrels, to fast-food mix-ups, to car sickness, to disgruntled car-seat captives. Not to mention the necessary paraphernalia that accompanies the journey: diapers, wipes, binkies, blanky, lovey, Desitin, Dimetapp, Tylenol, medicine dropper, thermometer, clothes, baby shampoo, teething ring, Orajel, Cheerios, bottles or sippy cups, baby spoons, bibs, stroller, port-a-crib, crayons, coloring books, toys, and, according to

Murphy's law, a cooler filled with ice in which to keep the inevitable bottle of Amoxicillin.

Of course, the older kids add their own brand of fun to the journey. They frequently have to go potty (or at least to explore the bathrooms of *every* restaurant and gas station along the way). While at the gas station, Dad simply *must* run inside for two-gallon cherry slurpees, which means another stop down the road for cleanup and at least a couple more to relieve bulging bladders. Little boys will also want to stop and leave their sunny yellow auto-graphs in pee at regular intervals along the highway.

I remember so vividly the experience of long-distance car trips with kids that just last Christmas I backed out of a "family" ski trip to Utah, at the last minute choosing instead to let the guys get away alone for some male bonding. You say I've become weak-hearted. I say I've embraced reality: kids in car seats on trips that take longer than four episodes of *Blues Clues* and moms over thirty-seven don't mix. I just couldn't scrape up the strength and patience required to play peek-a-boo, read *Pat the Bunny,* sing "Itsy Bitsy Spider," execute amusing facial contor-tions, and distribute Cheerios for ten hours straight. I used to think my husband was being heroic by insisting on manning the wheel for the whole trip, even driving all night sometimes. What a man! Finally I caught on. Whoever's driving doesn't have to referee and keep the kids entertained.

Last year, I was scheduled to do a speaking engagement about five hours north of where we live. My husband made great plans for the whole family to make the trek up to the San Joaquin Valley. Of course, the alternative was for him to keep all the kids and for me to go alone. I even offered to take all the boys and the breast pump, leaving him home with just eight-month-old Charli (I was still getting the easier end of the deal). He wasn't biting.

The day of departure arrived, and Chip had his bag packed. The boys threw their things in the van. I reluctantly threw in the virtual army trunk of aforementioned baby equipment thinking, "This is going to be a *long* trip. By tomorrow when I have to speak, my brain will most assuredly have turned to mush." But I sucked it up and buckled myself in for a wild ride.

We had to turn around and go home twice to retrieve forgotten necessities before we even got a mile away. Then we stopped for gas, then at a fast-food place for burgers. By the time we merged onto the freeway just blocks from the burger place, kids were complaining about screwed-up food orders, soda had been spilled, and the baby had started to cry. Before I could even process my thoughts, I screamed out, "Can we just go home?" Twenty minutes later, I was cheerfully heading up the 405 toward Fresno with my delightful eight-year-old escort Chandler while everyone else was back home, arguing over who had to eat the cheeseburger with mayonnaise.

The thing that keeps our foot on the gas and our eyes glued to the mile markers on any road trip is the destination at the other end. You know from the outset that things very likely won't go exactly as planned. There could be road construction along the way. You may get a flat tire. Someone might get carsick. There *will* be detours. At some point, you'll probably throw up your hands and blurt out, "Can we just go home?" Maybe you'll have to start back at square one and make some adjustments before proceeding. But there is a destination awaiting you. You can see it on the map. So you keep on driving.

Is there a personal goal you've set for yourself, some destination you've marked on the map, but you feel like calling off the trip? There've been too many setbacks, too much discouragement, too long a drive with too little progress to show for it. Thomas Edison himself admitted to thousands of failed experiments before finally perfecting the wonderful little invention we know today as the light bulb. Ray Charles, legendary blues singer and musician, kept right on pounding the ivories, even after being informed by his teachers that he had no talent and should find another way to support himself. When Anita Roddick was given the thumbs-down by numerous cosmetic manufacturers, she refused to turn back and eventually produced her own line of cosmetics and opened a chain of stores worldwide. Ever heard of The Body Shop?

In the famous words of Winston Churchill, set forth in his famous 1941 speech at Harrow School where he almost flunked out three times, "Never give in. Never give in. Never, never, never, never."

Don't give up on your goal, girlfriend. Keep your eye on the map and your foot on the gas. The day will come when you'll pull into your destination, and when you do—*celebrate* with a big two-gallon cherry slurpee on me!

On Family Pets

Our family loves pets. However, an all-points bulletin has been issued throughout the animal kingdom: "Do *not* under any circumstances go home with the Johnson family. Hop, crawl, or run like the wind." For some mysterious reason, death, illness, or extreme weirdness seems to befall every animal we adopt.

It started with Chile the wiener dog, whose first few weeks in our home is a blur. I remember days and nights filled with basically two things: Chile pooping in the kennel and Chile whining. Chile jumped off the couch one day while chewing a stick, and the stick went through the top of his head, exacerbating his already bizarre behavior. He whined at the door constantly. He peed on my neighbor's leg and on her freshly bathed dog twice. After that, I'd see her from a distance trying to teach Chile to sit when he'd run to greet her. At least it looked like that's what she was saying: "Oh, sit, Chile. Sit." After two years of increasingly strange behavior, we found Chile a new home with a nice lady who had all the time in the world to take him to therapy. "No more animals," I said.

Then Chase won a fish at a carnival. I hadn't yet learned that carnival fish last about as long as the carnival, so when he died we had to go to the pet store and buy a replacement. As I was cleaning Sam's bowl one day, he (or she—who can tell?) slipped past the strainer and disappeared down the drain. I was preparing to take the plumbing apart under the sink and rescue my son's little friend when suddenly a geyser of scalding water from the dishwasher exploded up through the pipes into the sink and poached Sam (or Samantha). "No more animals," I said.

Shortly thereafter, we went to the pet store just to look around, mind you, and came home with a gecko whom the boys named Timmy. One day, three-year-old Chandler accidentally grabbed Timmy by the tail. That lizard hung in midair for a split second, then fell to his cage below, leaving Chandler holding his tail. Timmy, being the sensitive reptile he was, seemed unable to cope emotionally with the stub that remained on his backside. He was laid to rest in a closed-shoe-box funeral a few days later. "No more animals," I said.

Then we got Chewy the mouse. We even bought him a brother named Charley so he wouldn't be lonely. We should have intervened early on, but we just chalked up their aggressive wrestling to the old "brothers will be brothers" routine—until one morning I found Chewy decapitated. I promptly traded that murderous mouse for two more who were actually siblings by birth (like that means they'll fight less?). We grew attached to the sisters, but after having them only a few weeks, they simultaneously began to move in slow motion like little wind-up toys one afternoon and died right there before our very eyes. "No more animals," I said.

Next came Lola the rat. I detested rats, couldn't stand them. But Lola changed all that. She was a beautiful blonde rat with the sweetest personality. She'd jump up on the side of the cage when we walked in the room so we'd reach in and scratch her belly. She loved to fall asleep in our hands as we stroked her fur. Lola and I bonded. One morning, after having Lola for only a few months, I walked into the room to find her lying lifeless on the floor of her condo. "No more animals," I said.

Prefaced by the words, "We're just going to look. We won't be bringing home a dog today," a visit to the local animal shelter smashed my resolution to bits. Bogey stood there amid all those highly spirited (that is, psycho) dogs as calm as could be, his kind eyes and wagging tail just begging for a new family. He was everything we wanted in a dog: mellow, loving, housebroken. He also had no front teeth, horrendous breath, unrelenting flatulence, and couldn't run to fetch a ball if his life depended on it. You see, Bogey had entered his golden years, but having fallen in love with him at first sight, we adopted him anyway. Two years later, Bogey began losing control of all his bodily functions, and we had to put him to sleep. Our hearts were broken.

Chance and I cried and hugged. "Mom," he sobbed, "we only had him for two years." The words formed in my heart and slowly made their way to my mouth, "Yes, honey, but weren't those two great years!" We agreed that the short time we had with stinky, toothless Bogey was well worth the tears and sadness on the day he left us.

That's why we keep setting ourselves up for heartache. Because the joy is worth the possibility of loss, of pain, of disappointment, we could say, "No more!" and really *mean* it. We've all been there. Someone we love has hurt us, and we declare, "No more! Never again will I give up a piece of my heart!"

In a song titled "The Dance," Garth Brooks sings of sharing a dance on a starry night, holding in his arms the woman he loves and later loses. If he'd known how it was going to end, would he have loved so freely? Bearing the scar from a broken heart, he savors the memories of earlier times and resolves, "I could have missed the pain, but I'd have had to miss the dance."

I'd better sign off now and go feed Max. Yep, that's right. We did it again, this time a neurotic but adorable mini-Schnauzer puppy that thinks our sole purpose in life is to love on him. It's great fun for all to watch him chase our giggling baby-girl Charli through the living room. So I guess "No more animals" is simply another way to say, "Give me some time to heal and then watch me jump right back in headfirst." After all, I can't miss the dance.

On Laundry

It dawned on me at some point that the only way I'll ever get my laundry caught up is if my family spends two days in the nude. As long as there are people living in this house, there will be a constant presence of laundry (unless we decide in the future to break with convention and start our own nudist colony).

It seems odd to me that the individuals who do not *do* the laundry (that is, everyone except me) appear to be the ones most conscientious about having clean clothes. I'm sure that's the case because when I gently remind them, "Pick your clothes up off the floor," they toss the whole bunch in the hamper to be washed. I'd like to think that this is a function of their pride in personal appearance rather than of being too lazy to fold the barely worn shirts and put them back in the dresser.

I, on the other hand, don't believe in indiscriminately tossing clothes into the hamper. That's like volunteering for overtime with no pay. If there are no visible stains and it passes the sniff test, back into the closet it goes. The same for towels. What's up with throwing a towel in the hamper after one use? My husband (who thinks clean towels magically appear and multiply in the linen closet) selects a fresh towel before every shower. I say if the towel gets dirty from drying off after a shower, you're not taking a very good shower, now are you?

I set myself up for frustration every time I flip open the lid of the washer and throw in a load of whites that includes the ever-elusive umpteen jillion pair of socks. No matter how many I throw in, when it comes folding time the numbers never match up. Socks are like the Holy Grail of laundry. If just once *all* matches to *every* pair of socks could make it through the dryer, I would know that a perfect world could not be far behind.

The single most dreaded category of laundry is stomach flu laundry. You can't just leave it until a more convenient time for obvious reasons, so you're forced to drop whatever else you were doing (probably sleeping, since these incidents usually occur around 2 A.M.) and begin stripping sheets and carefully transporting both them and their contents to the washer. As if that weren't enough, you have to rinse off, well, the big chunks by hand. You don't want them floating freely in the wash. So here you've already got a multiphase cleanup procedure before you even get the stuff into the washer. After four kids (and two gastrointestinally challenged wiener dogs), I still gag when I have to tackle stomach flu laundry.

Beach laundry runs a close second. I've braced myself for the day when the authorities come pounding on my door: "Mrs. Johnson, if your children will simply return the beach to its original location, no charges will be filed." How they can accumulate so much sand in such tiny clothes is a mystery to me. We shake and dump before heading home, but when I begin sorting laundry, there it is— my own little piece of the tropics. All that's missing is an umbrella and a beach ball. Incidentally, this scenario is played out almost exactly the same when replacing the word *beach* with *park*.

For all my complaining, I actually gain a sense of satisfaction from doing laundry. It's so cool how something can be thrown into the washer caked with squashed banana and strained peas and come out looking good as new. It's like that piece of clothing got a fresh start, a second chance. We don't toss our clothes in the trash just because they're dirty. That's what the washer's for.

Wouldn't it be great if there were a washer for our lives? We could pull off our socks that are soiled with failure and our sweats stained with screw-ups, throw them in the sudsy water, and come back in thirty minutes to find fresh-smelling new clothes to slip on.

In one of the most often-told parables of the Bible, Jesus tells the story of a young man who goes to his father and asks for his portion of the inheritance so that he can leave home and find himself. The father grants the son's request and off goes the young man to taste life in the big city, as it were. Soon he's spent everything on Jack Daniels, Rent-a-Date, and slot machines and has not one red cent remaining for a Big Mac. He finds himself working on a farm, so hungry that he snags some of the slop from the pigs. Then it hits him. "Here I am starving to death when all I ever needed is back at home. I'll return home and tell Dad I'm sorry for my foolishness and that if he'll just take me back, I'll settle for being one of his servants."

Rehearsing his plea for mercy as he journeys home, at last the son hits the driveway and his heart begins to race. "What if he won't take me back? He has every right not to after the stupid things I've done." Then in the distance he sees a man coming toward him—probably a servant leaving to do business. The figure draws closer. It's not a servant at all. It's his father. And he's running. Running with open arms to greet the son who separated himself from the family, who threw away his inheritance in no time on worthless pursuits and who now returns, ashamed and begging just to become a hired hand so he can feed himself.

The father throws his arms around the son known as "the prodigal," places a gold ring on his finger, a coat on his back, and some new shoes on his feet. Then he tops it off with a huge dinner party to celebrate the return of the son he'd waited for so long.

The picture this story paints is one of grace: a loving father, arms outstretched, running to greet us as soon as we start down the driveway toward home. Regardless of what we've done, he'll have no part of us coming on as a hired hand. No, he sits us down at the dinner table and says, "You're my child. All I have is yours."

Grace means God doesn't give up on us and throw us out because we're covered in mud. On the contrary, he longs for us to throw up our hands and call out to him, "Help! I'm a mess!" It means we can't do anything to make him love us more or anything to make him love us less. It means there's hope for the stinky, the sticky, and the stained laundry of our lives. There really is a second chance. That's the thing about laundry.

On Nursing

I began to think about weaning my baby-girl Charli when she was a year old, about the same age as her three older brothers had been when I closed up shop. But every time told myself, "Tonight will be the last nursing session," I'd become teary-eyed and rush to feed her before I dried up like the Sahara Desert—much different than in times past when a missed feeding meant an impending flood to rival that of Noah's big day.

I remember praying that my nursing pads were in optimum working order, as that familiar "let-down" sensation kicked in, signaling dinner time. Actually, it could be triggered not just at chow time but at any time by any number of things: a passing thought of how baby and daddy are doing at home, hearing another baby cry, or even a hug from a friend! That's all it took for my overzealous milk glands to jump to attention and yell, "Hit it boys— we're on!" Even now (and I hesitate to say this for fear of lighting a spark of envy in moms everywhere), I can milk my armpit. Yes, that's right—my armpit. Don't think I haven't contemplated turning a profit from it.

Nursing pads never really did the trick for me. They were immediately soaked, leaving me damp, sticky, and susceptible to that unpleasant sour-milk smell that tends to set in on a warm day. And they stubbornly refused to stay put inside my sexy flap-n'-snap nursing bra. Once after grocery shopping, I realized one of my nursing pads had worked its way out and was resting comfortably on my shoulder blade.

Imagine my excitement upon discovering a revolutionary new product called nursing cups! They resemble something a space princess from Star Trek might wear—two curved pieces of hard, round plastic that fit together to form a cup. In the middle of the bottom piece is a small, round hole so that theoretically the dripping milk would all be caught in the cup. Much to my disappointment, aside from the benefit of an extra cup size (literally), these things were duds. Any variation from the military "at attention" posture, and the milk came spilling out. Just as disconcerting, the cups created a sort of greenhouse effect on certain strategic body parts.

Missed feedings were enough to make me rethink ever being separated from my babies. One time, a good friend offered to watch my five-month-old while I went with my husband on a two-day ski trip. After a day without nursing, I felt like someone had blown up two huge party balloons inside my chest—a poster girl for cosmetic surgery gone bad. Fearing my rock-hard bosom would surely pop at any moment, I made a mad dash for the women's restroom in the lodge, peeled off the layers of clothes, stood over the toilet, and aimed. For more than twenty-five minutes, the distinct, rhythmic "swish, swish, swish" of milk hitting water echoed from my stall. I can only imagine what the ladies in that restroom were thinking.

Eventually, I obtained an electric pump. Its sound, reminiscent of a foghorn's "whaaa-whaaa-whaaa," lends that magical touch to any postpartum romantic getaway. And it's quite the handy little

gadget. Late one night on the way home from a conference about two hours north of my home, I conve-
niently pumped all the way down the 405 freeway,
only to discover that my batteries were low and there
were a whopping three drops of milk in the bottle. A
quick change of batteries and I was good to go. I
dumped five ounces of relief into my half-empty
Starbucks cup and switched sides, praying that I
would not get stopped by a police officer. I did have
a back-up plan, however, just in case. I would roll
down my window with a smile, grab the Starbucks
cup, and offer cheerfully, "Latte, officer?"

Considering the fact that a breast pump can be
used as an effective substitute for an industrial-
strength vacuum cleaner, it does have its downside.
Quite frankly, it did things to my anatomy I'd never
have imagined could be done except with Silly Putty.
Does the phrase "32 long" mean anything to you?

Don't get me wrong. Nursing was a *mostly*
wonderful experience. But I'll admit there were
many times it drained me dry, literally and figura-
tively. Was it worth the pain, the time, the mammary
reconfiguration, the embarrassing moments? Without a doubt—*Yes!*

Anything in life that's worthwhile comes at a
cost. I know it's quite a leap from nursing to Mother

Teresa, but stick with me. In 1948, Mother Teresa left the sheltered world of a convent to work among the poor of Calcutta, India. She traded the uniform of the order of Loreto for the customary garments of the poor among whom she would live and serve. Millions have benefited from works begun by Mother Teresa from orphanages to food kitchens, hospices for the dying to schools for the underprivileged. When the Nobel Peace Prize was presented to Mother Teresa in 1965, her life was described as one of "strict poverty and long days and nights of toil." Was it worth it? Would she do it over again? Her words leave no doubt as to the answers. "I see God in every human being. When I wash the leper's wounds, I feel I am nursing the Lord himself. Is it not a beautiful experience?"

What price have you paid this week for doing what's best for your family? Hang in there and stretch, girlfriend! You won't regret it.

On Public Humiliation

I'll never forget the day I walked out on the front porch of our town home to find three-year-old Chandler wearing nothing but a guitar, singing his lungs out to the neighborhood, "Jesus is just all right with me!" I admired his zeal, but his methodology teetered on the bounds of impropriety. We parents learn early in the game that the words *dignity, privacy,* and *discretion* are not even in the same dictionary as the word *children.*

The other evening, our long-time friend Andrew came to visit. We were relaxing, enjoying our after-dinner conversation, when suddenly my middle son comes bounding into the kitchen. "Mom, Mr. Maxi-Pad's been at it again!" Max, whose goal in life is to live up to my husband's nickname for him, has a sick obsession with used feminine hygiene products. When Chance discovered that Max had yet again made a disgusting mess on the carpet, he apparently saw no reason whatsoever why such a normal occurrence should not become a matter of public record. I thought about making a joke of it: "Guess who's not pregnant!" Instead, I turned as red as the mess Max had made, retrieved the carpet cleaner from under the sink, made my way past our blushing male guest, and dashed from the room.

It does my heart good in a demented sort of way to hear stories of other parents who've been similarly embarrassed by their children. Like four-year-old Theo, whose family was having dinner at a friend's house (why is it always at dinner?). The curious little guy, having been admiring the ceramic cow creamer on the table for some time, finally picked it up, turned it over, and examined it in earnest. "This cow has many penises," he observed matter-of-factly. That's what I call an ice-breaker.

Bodily functions also hold great fascination for kids. As if to say, "I've won the Nobel Peace Prize" they proudly announce in the middle of the restaurant, "I need to go poo-poo, Mommy." Not only are their own exploits proclaimed, they also feel the freedom to share news about mommy and daddy's otherwise private excretions. Like darling little Sarena, who told friends of the family, "Yesterday Daddy did a stinking toot-toot." Or my charming Chandler, who broadcast gleefully in numerous public restrooms, "Mommy, I do the poo-poo dance for you."

Church has always been a favorite forum in which my children consistently keep me humble. My oldest told his Sunday School teacher in second grade, "If Arnold Schwarzenegger and Sylvester Stallone are not going to be in heaven, then I don't want to go there either." Each of the three boys, exploring the easy maneuverability and exceptional aim capabilities of his urinary apparatus, has been spotted in years past relieving himself at various locations on the church grounds. And one Sunday evening when the pastor said, "Now, we'll have Sharon, our pianist, come and play," my young son said, within earshot of several parishioners, "Mom, he called Sharon a penis."

Tales of parental embarrassment of excremental proportions could fill countless volumes. However, my friend Sheila's story deserves special recognition. Heading home from a morning at the mall, Sheila got on the elevator with her little girls,

Madyson and Kayla. The shiny steel doors slid shut, and down they went. An odor immediately began to fill the tiny enclosure. A little embarrassing gas. Luckily they were alone. Then the elevator stopped and an impeccably dressed woman who could have stepped straight off the cover of *Vogue* appeared in the fog. Since there was no denying the obvious air-quality problem, Sheila offered politely, "Sorry about the smell."

All would have been fine had it not been for Kayla's keen sense of sight. "Mommy, Madyson went poo-poo. Look." There on the floor, in a shape reminiscent of a snowman, was the source of the stench. Sheila pretended not to hear and commenced a loud one-way conversation with her daughters to disguise Kayla's ongoing announcement, "Mommy, look, Madyson's poo-poo is on the floor. Are you going to clean it up?" The thought was racing through Sheila's mind: "What is Vogue Lady over here thinking—that I *let* my daughter poop on the floor and simply shrugged it off with a meager, 'Sorry about the smell'?" The doors opened once again. Mortified and beyond all hopes of recapturing some sense of dignity, Sheila backed the gargantuan double stroller out of the reeking elevator, squashing the snowman as she exited and leaving a Hansel-and-Gretel trail behind her as she bolted for her minivan. I must say, to her immense credit, she did regain composure and went back to clean up the dump site.

Children are born with a mission: to keep parents humble. It's difficult to maintain a high-and-mighty attitude when at any moment your toddler may squat down in the book store and begin grunting or your preschooler may ask loudly and with all sincerity, "Mommy, why is that lady's hair blue?" Interestingly, the word *humility* comes from the Latin *humus,* which means lowly and "of the earth."

There is another *"hum"* word that is like a fabric softener that helps us slip more comfortably into the potentially stiff and scratchy down-to-earth coat of humility. Our healthiest response to innocent offspring embarrassments is to face them head-on with a sense of humor. People who don't take themselves or their children's inevitable "pick the nose and eat it" incidents too seriously have an ease about them that allows others to loosen up and laugh as well. They are approachable, relatable, and (not coincidentally) some of the most humble folks you'll meet. Their sense of humor has enabled them to snuggle into their coat of humility and break it in like an old pair of blue jeans.

Remember, next time your adorable angel lets loose a window-rattling toot, causing everyone in line at the bank to simultaneously shoot mortified glances your way, one day the tables will turn. There'll be unsolicited kisses on the cheek as you drop him off at junior high school, albums teeming with bare-bottom baby photos to pull out whenever that potential boy- or girlfriend comes to call, and school dances where you'll be overtaken with rhythm and compelled to do the bump with every other chaperone at the punch bowl. Take it from the mother of a teenager: it's a great feeling to present a nice, down-to-earth coat of humility to the sweetie who slipped one on your own shoulders not so long ago.

On Dog Food and Empty Boxes

I'm firmly convinced that the reason toy companies work feverishly to crank out new-and-improved, better-than-ever toys of all shapes, sizes, and sorts is that they want to divert us from learning the truth. Kids can and *will* make their own toys out of anything they find lying around the house. Every family photo album contains pictures of Junior sitting contentedly in an empty box while his brand new scooter sits unoccupied somewhere in the background. The box is the real unexplored treasure.

A few years ago, we bought a new TV—one of those huge TVs that shouts, "A manly man lives here!" It came in a sturdy, gargantuan box that our kids went nuts over. They piled toys, pillows, and blankets in that thing, and every day they argued over who got to sleep in the box that night. The TV was OK, but that box was the *real* deal.

Charli has found an unexpected pastime using something we would have never thought of as having recreational potential: dog food. She methodically places each individual piece into Max's water bowl, removes it, and puts it back into the food bowl, a little soggier than Max likes it but fascinating for Charli just the same. Did I mention that when the food is still crunchy, Charli enjoys a nibble here and there? I must say her hair has become much shinier since we got Max.

This industrious daughter of mine also loves to empty the bottom cabinets of Tupperware and parade around with various colorful bowls on her head. Why wouldn't she? They are the perfect shape to sit teetering atop a toddler's head. She actually has a talent for making a hat out of most anything— her brothers' boxer shorts, napkins, a small trash can. She'll wear anything *but* an actual hat.

One day while shopping at Target with Charli, I learned by accident that those round multicolored stickers in the office supply aisle possess far more potential than we give them credit for. Normally used for color-coding files and such, this particular day I hurriedly grabbed them without much thought and handed them to Charli, grasping for anything to keep her occupied until I could check off the last few items on my list. Charli recognized what I had never seen: these stickers make superior hair accessories and serve as festive temporary facial decorations. I was the envy of all the other shoppers with my neon-green cheeks and fluorescent-orange bangs. Back at home, Max the dog was not quite as enthusiastic as I to be the recipient of Charli's exciting new discovery.

My friend has an incredibly visionary little boy named Max, who continually amazes with his ability to squeeze every drop of potential from his surroundings. One day, his mother, Mary, walked into her dining room to find two-year-old Max swinging from the chandelier. Of *course* he was swinging from the chandelier. It was shiny, curious, and just hanging there begging to be engaged by a budding Tarzan. This same little preschooler can often be found in his backyard in the nude, creating beautiful tempera paint masterpieces. No object is the sum total of its appearance for Max. A canister vacuum becomes a fireman's hose. Videotape cases become shin guards for a suit of armor. Max is a modern-day, pint-sized "Renaissance man."

Nothing lies outside a child's knack for transforming the common into the novel. Right now, I'm forced to wear one black, furry house slipper and one white, flowered house slipper because my sons have used their mates to practice skateboard moves in the house. They jump off couches, stairs, whatever space is available, flipping the slippers in the air and "landing" their tricks by grabbing the slippers as they ride them to the ground. Sometimes they maneuver a kickflip, and sometimes they bust a 360. To me they were just slippers.

The eyes of a child can look upon the most common of everyday objects and infuse them with limitless potential—"outside the box" potential, so to speak. What if we looked through their lenses for a while? Remember when you first laid eyes on your child? She was a brand new treasure to behold. You really didn't know what to expect. You just let her be who she was and took it all in. Somewhere along the way, we develop rather fixed expectations of what they will say and do. We can almost predict their responses.

What if we look at our children today as if they had just been placed in our arms—these miraculous creatures of boundless possibility? What if we allow ourselves to be swept away in the wonder of those first few weeks and months when every "first" was cause for celebration? When we set aside our preconceived notions of who they will be today, we begin to open up a whole world of magical possibility for them and for ourselves. After all, consider the potential of dog food and empty boxes.

On Postpartum Changes

Like lilies wilting in the noonday sun are the breasts of a postpartum woman. Mammary changes occur during gestation that bestow upon even the most diminutive of women a colossal case of cleavage. If pregnancy hormones could be bottled and sold, cosmetic surgeons and silicone implant manufacturers everywhere would go out of business. However, you know the old saying: "What goes up . . ."

For those who enter pregnancy possessing an ample bosom, the postpartum period ushers in a dramatic southern relocation of the bustline. My friend Carla summed it up aptly: "These boobs nursed two children. They *deserve* a rest."

For those like myself who are of slighter build (we owe our only discernible chest protrusions to the fabulous Wonder Bra), it is likewise impossible to retain any semblance of prepregnancy perkiness. Perhaps it is best explained thusly. Suppose you take an eight-inch balloon and blow it up to its fullest capacity without it popping, say, to about eleven inches. Imagine that you keep that balloon stretched to its max for about a year or so. Maybe for good measure, you grab the end of the balloon with your teeth and give it several really good, long tugs throughout the day and night. Then one day you release enough air from the balloon to bring it back down to its original petite eight-inch size. Only now your bouncy, round, taut balloon droops despondently, having lost all elasticity and memory of how to behave as an eight-inch balloon. Its new shape, particularly from certain vantage points, is best described as tubular. Add several well-placed stretch-marks, and that is the plight of the postpartum, petite-chested woman.

Another benefit of carrying and birthing babies is the ability to urinate freely at any given moment with little-to-no effort. Since giving birth to my children, my greatest fear is sneezing in public. I've become much more graceful, avoiding even the slightest jarring of the bladder. The realization that my urinary stamina had diminished drastically occurred when I had to cut short one of my first postpartum trips to the gym after only three jumping jacks. Having foolishly positioned myself on the front row of the aerobics class, I could only hope that the participants to my rear were too engrossed in their work-out to notice the dripping as I dashed from the room.

We've all been handed the line that doing Kegels during pregnancy will prevent incontinence, but the ten or twelve that I pulled off did absolutely no good whatsoever. It seems to me that expecting a pelvic exercise to prevent a leaky bladder during pregnancy is like expecting a used Band-Aid to hold back the Hoover Dam.

With pregnancy also comes the gift of an extra stash of skin. Personally, I think it's rather handy, especially in sudden rainstorms. No umbrella? No problem. I just reach down and grab a handful of hide near my bellybutton, pull it up and over my head, and I'm dry as can be. If I retain a slightly bent-over position, I can carry extra pencils and a lipliner in the folds of skin.

Stretchmarks and varicose veins are yet another visible reminder of my miraculous birthing experiences. They can provide hours of entertainment for the kids. I just give them some markers, write Start Here on the upper thighs and End Here around the ankles, tell them to follow the lines, and off they go.

Every day, my feet remind me of the four extra loads they were called on to carry for months on end. I would hesitate to mention this, but I've heard it from so many other moms, I figure I must not be a lone freak. Since carrying child number one, I have enjoyed the distinction of possessing a left-shoe size 5 and 1/2 and a right-shoe size 6. And my already-protruding bunions took on a life of their own, demanding to be adorned with open sandals or wide, clunky clogs, no matter the season or occasion.

Finally, I'm not sure exactly what has happened to my uterus and various nearby organs, but I know parts have begun peeking out that before childbirth had never seen the light of day. Again, this may prove beneficial in simplifying the whole gynecological exam procedure. No more probing and squinting. Everything is easily visible and accessible.

I guess it's a pretty fair assessment to say that the process of growing, carrying, and bringing a new little life into the world can cause monumental physical changes. Some I don't mind so much; others—well, quite frankly, I'm not so thrilled about. But all in all, I'm enormously grateful that my body spared no expense in doing what it needed to do in order to gift me with these children.

One day, I sat down and wrote a song to encourage not only my fellow moms but every woman out there who is bombarded constantly with images of unrealistic physical perfection on every side: billboards, TV, magazines, you name it. Part of it goes like this:

Well, my body's not the same as it was before these kids
Some things don't seem to work the way they always did
Some parts got bigger; others vanished clean away
Well I'm no supermodel, but I'm just fine this way
I have finally seen the light
That's not me, but that's all right

If you've given birth to a child, your body has served as honored host to a precious miracle. Even if you haven't birthed a child, your body in and of *itself* is miraculous! It will continue to collect keepsakes through the years—laugh lines from watching your two-year-old hobble down the hall in your shoes, a wrinkle or two from waiting up for teenagers, grey hairs that proudly announce, "I've been there for many a grandchild's birthday party!" And perhaps the honorable signatures of childbirth. Your body is a testament to life—and that's absolutely, positively, *all right!*

On Picture Day

If you've got kids, you've done picture day. And if you're like me, each time you swear it will be the last. What begins as a naïve attempt to dress everyone in their Sunday best and capture a memory for posterity often evolves into a harrowing afternoon of crying, fighting, and refusing to strike the required Cleaver family pose. And that's just the husbands.

It is impossible, not *nearly* impossible or *virtually* impossible but *absolutely impossible* to get *everyone* sitting still in one place with clean clothes, combed hair, and Kodak-moment smiles. One of our very first family picture experiences after our third son came along was the catalyst for my husband's

solemn vow: "I will *never* do this again." I guess
somewhere between the two-hour wait (during
which we played every game imaginable, distributed
no less than ten pounds of Cheerios, and chased the
little sprinters up and down the mall at least fifty
times) and the actual sitting (which should have
been called a squirming), he just snapped. After a
year or so, I convinced him that in fact family pictures are a necessary part of life and that if we didn't
have them taken at least two times before the kids
were grown, we would make the cover of *World's
Worst Parents.*

My friend Lynette's story captures the essence
of picture day. She and her husband were taking
their two-month-old baby for her first pictures since
the hospital. All dressed in her frilly finest, little
blonde-haired Brooke outshined the brightest angel.
There she lay, serenely gracing mommy's arms as the
photographer counted, "One, two . . ." Right on cue,
itty-bitty Brooke let loose and let 'er fly. Up and out
of her ruffled panties came a yellow, oozing, noxious
substance to rival anything Steven Spielberg could
concoct. The gagging photographer was aghast.

My utterly flustered friends ran out to purchase the first baby outfit they could find and then
rushed into the ladies' bathroom—*all* of them . . .

Brooke, Mommy, *and Daddy!* In the case of rookie parents, it is often necessary to employ the buddy system in dealing with messes of this magnitude. Apparently, the situation did not seem at all under control to the elderly lady in the restroom who kindly asked, "Would you kids like some help?" Brooke put her special signature on that outfit as well—and on the next, before finally wrapping up picture day.

As we parents are fully aware, the sitting is only half the picture-day experience. The viewing of the portraits is a whole different deal. You have to come back another day and watch as the salesperson masterfully creates a grand layout of photographs—precious snapshots capturing the likeness of your cherished treasures. Your job is to decide which ones you will purchase (after all, they're priceless) and which of these heirlooms you will leave with these complete strangers to be carelessly tossed in the shredder.

The basic package you initially came in for is *only* $29.95: a couple of 8 by 10s, fifty wallets, and twenty thumbnail-size photos that no one has ever figured out what to do with. But the pose in which Jimmy is *not* picking his nose and almost everyone's eyes are *open* is *never* included in that package. You may, however, purchase these beautiful portraits (the "best of the portfolio") for an additional cost of *only* $50 per sheet. You *do* buy them of course, because, after all, the kids are only this age once, and they really are so doggone cute that you want to present them in their best light, which seems to entail them *not* picking their noses. And really, the family does appear to be more friendly in the $50 pose than in the package shot where Mom and Dad are seething through clenched teeth, "Timmy, stop pinching your sister right now and smile!" So out comes the credit card, and off you prance with the picking-the-nose packet *and* the "best of the portfolio," soon to be framed and displayed in a place of prominence— announcing to all who enter your home, "This is my family, my pride and joy. Aren't they great!" This is why we do picture day.

We parents treasure photographs of our children because they are a representation of those little people we love so much, not because of their accomplishments (for how much can a three-month-old really aspire to?) or their exemplary behavior (as any mother of a two-year-old can attest). They don't have to earn our love. They are precious to us simply because they are our children.

How wonderful to be on the receiving end of that kind of love! That's how freely God loves us. Sometimes I forget that. I work furiously to impress him under the misguided notion that he'll say, "Oh, now I *really* love you. Now you *deserve* all of my love." That's just *not* how it is with God. When I pass by my family portrait and take a long, proud look at those awesome kids of mine, the truth once again comes to rest in my heart. I am loved by God simply because I'm his child. As one writer put it, "If God had a wallet, *your* picture would be in it."

On Flying with Babies

Any parent who's flown with a baby has earned her wings in my book. It's not an easy undertaking. As soon as junior starts to cry, the steely glances of strangers speak loud and clear: "Can't you make him stop crying?" And heaven help you if the little darling makes a poopy. That elicits another set of stares altogether: "We don't care if the fasten-seatbelt sign is on. Go to the bathroom and change your kid's diaper!"—a ridiculous expectation, since there's barely room to hover perilously over the postage-stamp-sized toilet, much less to change a baby in an airplane lavatory.

My friend Donna was on a packed plane with her three-year-old daughter and baby boy when her little guy filled his diaper to overflowing. Up and out, all over his clothes it seeped, the stinky, gooey mess. Right beside Donna sat a big, burly man who, judging by the expression of disdain on his face, was clearly *not* a father. Not an ounce of sympathy softened his countenance as Donna was forced to kneel down in front of her seat, strip down her smelly son, use every last baby wipe cleaning up the toxic spill, dispose of the soiled clothes, and strap herself back in the seat with her half-naked son. You do what you gotta do.

I recall more than once spending half my flight in the back of the plane, bouncing a screaming baby while keeping a watchful eye out for my toddler up in the cabin. Once the seatbelt sign went on and the flight attendants kicked me out of the galley (you learn the lingo when you spend enough time back there), I returned to my seat and was forced to continue with a sitting bounce-rock combination which is, by the way, a marvelous alternative to traditional crunches and sit-ups for some serious ab work.

Friends and family members who've been on the receiving end of a mother flying alone with her kids know the drill. Their worn-out loved one will exit the plane, kids in tow, looking like a reject from "Night of the Living Dead." She will hold it together until they arrive at their final destination, at which point the depleted mother will hand the kids off to the nearest breathing human, stumble into the first bedroom she sees, lock the door, and collapse into a deep sleep.

I witnessed one of the most trying instances ever of flying with little ones a few months ago when I was returning home to Southern California. My heart still breaks for this nice couple who sat in front of me—a young family headed for a long-anticipated vacation to Disneyland with their two-year-old son and four-year-old daughter.

The kids had been doing great until we started to land. Their ears began to hurt, and they started to scream. The little boy was somewhat consolable, but the little girl became increasingly frantic, and her cries quickly turned into blood-curdling screams, "Mommy, I can't breathe, I can't breathe, I can't breathe!" Of course, she was hyperventilating from the screaming, but the poor mom could do nothing to calm her hysterical daughter. My heart ached, and I cried for this anguished mother who was helpless to stop the pain or the fear that consumed her little girl.

The genuine empathy from every parent on that plane was almost palpable, as the wailing of the little girl continued on and on. After what seemed like an eternity, at last we landed, and the little girl's screams subsided. The weary mother collapsed back in her seat and sobbed. I stood and reached over the seat, resting my hand gently on her shoulder, and said the only words that came to mind at the moment: "I know."

As this physically and mentally drained couple made their way down the narrow aisle with their children, I heard this conversation: "How are we going to get back home? There's no way we can get on a plane again." "I don't know. We'll figure something out."

Even now, I get a lump in my throat as I recall vividly the anguish of those young parents. Why? Because I've been there. When I placed my hand on my fellow mom's shoulder and said, "I know," I meant it. I've been on the receiving end of an empathetic hug, a word of encouragement, a timely note, a hand on the shoulder that says, without question, "I understand." It makes a difference. It means I'm not alone. Somebody else gets it.

When's the last time you heard the "I know" of a fellow mom? It's so important to spend time with others like ourselves who get it, who know firsthand this round-the-clock roller coaster of life with little people—the "I wouldn't trade this for anything"/ "Why did I ever have children?" ups and downs of mothering. We *need* to swap "Yeah, me too" stories, as my friend Stacy calls them.

If you don't have connections like this in your life, why not take the first step this week? There is probably a mom or two on your block who'd love to spend time with someone else who gets it. There are moms' groups in almost every community and even Internet resources to get you networked when you can't find a group in your area. I know it's difficult sometimes to venture out of the comfort zone, but it's well worth it when you tell your story of losing patience with your two-year-old that morning and blurting out a bad word and you hear another mom say with relief, "Yeah, me too." It's that hand on the shoulder that says, "I know." And she really does.

References

On Binkies
Cloud, H., and Townsend, J. *Boundaries with Kids*. Grand Rapids, Mich.: Zondervan, 1998, p. 52.

On Moms and Fashion Statements
Kushner, H. *When All You've Ever Wanted Isn't Enough*. New York: Pocket Books, 1986, p. 17.

On Sleep Deprivation
"Now may the God" (Romans 15:13).

On Oozing Poop
"Like apples of gold": (Proverbs 25:11).

On Colic
"God, my God, you have made me" (I Kings 3:7–9); Peterson, E. *The Message: The Bible in Contemporary Language*. Colorado Springs, Colo.: NavPress, 2002, p. 568.

On Sex After Kids
Lewis, C. S. *The Four Loves.* Orlando: Harcourt Brace, 1960, p. 116.

On Bathroom Matters
Hebrews 13:5,6.

On Labor Discomfort
Brand, as quoted in Yancey, P., *Where Is God When It Hurts?* Grand Rapids, Mich.: Zondervan, 1997, p. 65.

Yancey, p. 55.

"Blessed be the God and Father" (II Corinthians 1:3,4).

On Family Vehicles
Vaillant, G. E., M.D. *Surprising Guideposts to a Happier Life from the Landmark Harvard Study of Adult Development.* New York: Little, Brown, 2002.

On Owies
Harken, as quoted in Kersey, C. *Unstoppable.* Naperville, Ill.: Sourcebooks, Inc., 1998.

On Grocery Shopping with a Toddler
Muggeridge, as quoted in James B. Simpson (ed.), *Simpson's Contemporary Quotations.* Boston: Houghton-Mifflin, 1988.

On Family Pets
Arata, T. *The Dance.* Copyright 1989 by Morganactive Songs, Inc., Nashville (sung by Garth Brooks).

On Laundry
Luke 15:11–44.

On Nursing
"Mother Teresa: In Her Own Words." Available at www.washingtonpost.com, Sept. 5, 1997, copyright 1997 by the Associated Press.

On Picture Day
"You formed my inner parts" (Psalm 139:13,14, New Living Translation).

About the Author

Lisa Espinoza Johnson is a humorist, recording artist, writer, and speaker, with a B.A. in psychology and an on-the-job training certificate from the BTDT (been-there-done-that) School of Mothering. Her album, "Candy Kisses, Muddy Hugs," has been a source of encouragement for moms across the nation. A regular columnist for *Christian Parenting Today*, Lisa has also written for *MomSense* and *American Baby* magazines. She is a popular conference and retreat speaker, known for her down-to-earth humor and practical insight. Audiences consistently respond to Lisa's tell-it-like-it-is style with such comments as "inspiring," "encouraging," "hilarious," and "spoke to me right where I'm at." Lisa also holds the distinguished title of "Most Likely to Get Lost on the Way to Soccer Practice," as well as "Most Likely to Burn Chicken Nuggets—Every Time!" Her Web site is candykissesmuddyhugs.com.

Lisa and her husband, Chip, live in Southern California with their neurotic dog Max and their four energetic but not neurotic kids: three sons and the newest member of the family—a baby *girl!*

Get Connected

My lifeline through these years of mothering has been my connection with *other moms.* One of the primary ways I've been able to make those connections is through my involvement with MOPS (Mothers of Pre-Schoolers) International. When I went to my MOPS meeting each week, I got to sip my coffee while enjoying a speaker dealing with topics ranging from "how to know if your child is ready for potty training" to "planning a birthday party on a shoe-string" to "bolstering your self-esteem when you've got puke on your sleeve and Cheerios in your hair." I engaged in meaningful discussions with my fellow moms and heard *lots* of "Yeah, me too" stories. And I got to make a craft of some kind, finish it, and take it home. How often do we moms actually get to *finish* something in one sitting? All this while my kids were being well taken care of and having fun in their own special program called MOPPETS.

My experience with MOPS helped transform my whole perspective on mothering. Without a doubt, this book is a byproduct of the inspiration and encouragement I received from my fellow moms at MOPS.

MOPS groups meet in different churches all over the United States and in twenty other countries. If there's no MOPS group in your area, MOPS can still get you connected to other moms and offer support in a variety of ways. Their message is that "mothering matters." I got the message loud and clear.

Check out their Web site at www.MOPS.org or call 1–800–929–1287 to see how you can benefit from MOPS.

Another organization whose goal is to affirm moms is Hearts at Home (www.hearts-at-home.org). Their philosophy is that motherhood is a profession to be highly esteemed, and they seek to support and equip women in this monumental role of mothering. Hearts at Home holds conferences across the country, with seminars covering everything from "anger management for moms" to "once-a-month cooking." These conferences offer practical, hands-on tools for moms to use daily and act as a potent booster shot.

Whether you get connected with other moms through MOPS, Hearts at Home, your local play-group, or some other organization, the important thing is *get connected!* We need each other!